Pastor Kim Daniels' *Delivered to Destiny* is not just a book; it's an instruction manual and guide to excellence in spiritual warfare and deliverance that will result in an improved quality of life on earth and provide a pathway to increased power in Christ.

—MC HAMMER
HAMMER4G
FULLBLAST MUSIC GROUP

This is an incredible book! Reading it reminds me of God's power to love and reach anyone, no matter where you are and what you've done, so that your true purpose can be fulfilled.

—CECE WINANS
FIVE-TIME GRAMMY AWARD–WINNER AND
PLATINUM-SELLING RECORDING ARTIST

The story of God's amazing work in my friend Kim Daniels' pilgrimage is clearly one of the most incredible true-life demonstrations of the power of God I could ever imagine. *Delivered to Destiny* is one of those books you will have a hard time putting down. I love this book!

—C. PETER WAGNER, PRESIDING APOSTLE
INTERNATIONAL COALITION OF APOSTLES

This book is an amazing testimony to God's grace. God has a purpose and destiny for each individual. Those who feel too soiled by sin to ever be used in kingdom service will discover that no one need be a prisoner of his past, for we are new creations through Christ Jesus. God's grace is truly amazing!

—FRANK D. HAMMOND
BEST-SELLING AUTHOR, *PIGS IN THE PARLOR*
COFOUNDER, THE CHILDREN'S BREAD MINISTRY

A fearless and unpretentious woman of God has written a book that you won't be able to put down.

—R. T. KENDALL
BEST-SELLING AUTHOR AND SPEAKER
FORMER PASTOR, WESTMINSTER CHAPEL, LONDON, ENGLAND

DELIVERED TO
DESTINY

KIMBERLY DANIELS

Charisma
HOUSE
A STRANG COMPANY

Most STRANG COMMUNICATIONS/CHARISMA HOUSE/SILOAM products are available at special quantity discounts for bulk purchase for sales promotions, premiums, fund-raising, and educational needs. For details, write Strang Communications/Charisma House/Siloam, 600 Rinehart Road, Lake Mary, Florida 32746, or telephone (407) 333-0600.

DELIVERED TO DESTINY by Kimberly Daniels
Published by Charisma House
A Strang Company
600 Rinehart Road
Lake Mary, Florida 32746
www.charismahouse.com

Unless otherwise noted, all Scripture quotations are from the New King James Version of the Bible. Copyright © 1979, 1980, 1982 by Thomas Nelson, Inc., publishers. Used by permission.

Scripture quotations marked AMP are from the Amplified Bible. Old Testament copyright © 1965, 1987 by the Zondervan Corporation. The Amplified New Testament copyright © 1954, 1958, 1987 by the Lockman Foundation. Used by permission.

Scripture quotations marked KJV are from the King James Version of the Bible.

People and incidents in this book are composites created by the author from her life experiences. Names and details of the stories have been changed, and any similarity between the names and stories of individuals described in this book to individuals known to readers is purely coincidental.

Cover design by DogEared Design, Kirk DouPonce

Library of Congress Cataloging-in-Publication Data

Daniels, Kimberly.
  Delivered to destiny / Kimberly Daniels.
     p. cm.
  ISBN 1-59185-614-0 (pbk.)
  1. Daniels, Kimberly. 2. Christian biography--United States.
I. Title.
  BR1725.D33A3 2005
  269'.2'092--dc22

                                        2005005349

05 06 07 08 09 — 98765432
Printed in the United States of America

THIS BOOK IS DEDICATED TO THE MEMORY OF:

Derek Prince

Kenneth Hagin Sr.

Frank Hammond

Frank Marzullo

These mighty men of God pioneered deliverance
ministry and personally touched my life.

CONTENTS

Foreword by Diana Hagee...ix

Introduction 1

1   A Date With Destiny.. 9

2   Uptown Girl... 21

3   Uptown Roots... 33

4   Moving On Up!.. 49

5   Introduction to Witchcraft...57

6   I'm Coming Out!.. 65

7   From Crazy to the Crack House.. 77

8   Back With Danny.. 85

9   The Army Life.. 95

10 A Babe in Christ... 105

11 Times of Testing 113

12 Free Indeed 121

13 Desert Storm... 129

14 A Demon Buster Is Born... 137

15 Ordained and Activated 147

16 A New Season 153

17 In the Occult 161

18 Generational Blessings 169

19 It Should've Been Me... 179

20 From the Guttermost to the Uttermost 189

    My Confession of Faith... 195

FOREWORD

K IM IS A woman who knows the pain of losing a child, a loved one, a dream, and hope. She has seen her dream ebb away because of her addiction to drugs. But she has also witnessed God's promise to restore all that was stolen from her.

Pastor Hagee and I have had the privilege of hearing many testimonies over the course of our ministry, but Kim's life story is ranked among the best. To know Kim is to know someone who is genuine, who is godly, who has a wonderful sense of humor, and above all, who is a warrior for God. Her smile and passion for the Lord are contagious. She is aggressive in spiritual warfare because she knows what it is like to have the enemy steal everything from you.

Kim's story is one of adversity, tribulation, hope, and restoration. As you read it, she will make you laugh at times and at other times cry. Kim is very candid about her past, but it is not for the shock value. She is open with you about her past life to help you understand that God has truly delivered her into the destiny

He had planned for her. If He can deliver her from the gutter of despondency and despair to a fully restored life, then He will do the same for you. Regardless of your spiritual, physical, or financial status in life, Kim's life will touch you. You will be both encouraged and inspired by the power of God's transforming love as you read *Delivered to Destiny*.

—DIANA HAGEE

INTRODUCTION

S OME OF YOU may have read my original autobiography, *Against All Odds*, which focuses on "coming out" of bondage. It was a raw caption of my life, but *Delivered to Destiny* tells my entire life story. It promotes the principle of "going in" to what God desires for you.

In the body of Christ, we hear testimony after testimony of what people have overcome. In fact, millions of believers have been delivered from drug addiction, lust, greed, lying, adultery, and other vices. But *coming out* of sin is just the beginning for a believer.

For instance, all of the children of Israel came out of Egypt. The interesting thing about their deliverance is that only a portion of the ones who came out actually went into the Promised Land. As believers, we all must leave "Egypt" or the sins that hold us back in life. But be careful; the Bible warns us that the enemy comes immediately to steal the Word of God from our hearts. By this I mean he quickly comes to snatch our deliverance.

The wilderness, where the children of Israel spent forty years, is a very strategic place; it can be a blessing or a curse. It's like the valley of decision. The wilderness is a place where we decide to either submit to God or walk out our salvation as double-minded Christians.

According to Deuteronomy 11:29, God told the Hebrew children to possess the land. They would inhabit the land by separating the blessing from the curse. He told them to put the curse on Mt. Ebal and the blessing on Mt. Gerizim. The Hebrew meaning of *Ebal* is to be "bald; bare."

Gerizim, however, means to be "cut up and rocky." The "mountain of the curse" will manifest the smooth, easy, and comfortable way in life, but the "mountain of blessings" is rocky and hard. This is what makes the choice so difficult.

> GOD WILL NOT ONLY BRING YOU OUT OF THINGS YOU'RE BOUND TO, BUT HE WILL ALSO LEAD YOU INTO YOUR DESTINY.

The wilderness is a place where we can grow through our afflictions and be prepared to walk in divine destiny. But those who are not willing to suffer with Christ, who have only murmured and complained along the way, will not go in!

PURPOSE AND DESTINY

My deliverance from addiction and all the other horrors I came out of was not the end; it was the beginning! It's awesome! God will not only bring you out of things you're bound to, but He will also lead you into your destiny.

In order for you to understand my ministry and what I am called to do, it will help if you understand what God has brought me out of. But more important than my past is what He has taken me into—my destiny in Him!

Destiny is the root word for "destination," a place to where one is going or directed. Destiny is not limited to a place down the road, but according to *Webster's* dictionary, it is a predetermined course of events held to be an irresistible power. God is not just concerned about us fulfilling our destiny; He instead has a course mapped out for us to get there.

Purpose is the name of the road that leads us to our destiny. Many people focus on their *purpose*, but they never make it their *destination*. As you walk down the road of purpose, I pray that the obstacles of life will not hinder or stop you from reaching your destiny.

Don't allow what you have come out of to stop you from obtaining what God has prepared for you. Ephesians 1:11 says, "We have obtained an inheritance, being predestined according to the purpose of Him who works all things after the counsel of His own will." I have learned never to question the *way of God* as long as I can discern the *will of God* for my life. I take much comfort in knowing that whatever I go through—good or bad—God is there with me. As I walk in the will of God, I know I am not alone. Note Isaiah 63:9:

> In all their affliction He was afflicted,
> And the Angel of His Presence saved them;
> In His love and in His pity He redeemed them;
> And He bore them and carried them
> All the days of old.

The aforementioned scripture says His "presence" saved them. The Hebrew translation of *presence* is *pawneem*, and it means "the face," favor, or front part of God. Studying the phrases "angel of the Lord" and "Angel of His Presence" has taught me that this front part of God goes before us to show us the way to our destiny.

Even when we do not have all the details, God leads us in the way we are to go. This is why we must not lean to our own understanding, but acknowledge the Lord in all that we do. As a result, He will give us clear direction.

For instance, Moses was destined to deliver the children of Israel from Egypt, but he had no idea where to start. He began by asking God to "show him His glory." God said He could not show Moses His "front part," but that He would give him a glimpse of His back.

The "back part" of God represents prophecies and promises from God that have been revealed to the saints. The "front part" of God represents the things we cannot see and have to believe Him for. To further explain my point, look at Exodus 23:20–21 (KJV).

> Behold, I send an Angel before thee, to keep thee in the way, and to bring thee into a place which I have prepared. Beware of him, and obey his voice, provoke him not; for he will not pardon your transgressions: for my name is in him.

We have heard teachings on many types of angels. I call the angel spoken of in the above text, "the angel of destiny." We must be aware that angels are assigned to lead us into our destiny and to deliver us from whatever tries to keep us clutched in the enemy's stronghold. Praise God!

We have been brought out of sin to "go in" with God! God said that the destiny angel could not be provoked, because he had the name of God on the inside of him. The word *name* in this scripture in Hebrew is *shem*. When God used this word, He meant that this angel had the honor, authority, and character of God on the inside of him.

One of the Hebrew words for *angel* is *mal-ak*, which means "ambassador." An ambassador represents the authority of the president of a certain country. When the angel of the Lord is sent forth, he not only represents the authority of God, but he also has the honor and character of God. But we know that we should not worship angels or give them God's glory.

On the other hand, when God sends an angelic representation of Himself, we cannot take it lightly. He told Israel that if they were to be led by the angel of the Lord, obedience along the way would not be an option. Moses said he would not lead the children of Israel out of Egypt unless God went with him. God, in response, told Moses that He could not go with him, because the people were stiff-necked. God warned Moses that He would kill them before they reached their destination.

> Then the LORD said to Moses, "Depart and go up from here, you and the people whom you have brought out of the land of Egypt, to the land of which I swore to Abraham, Isaac, and Jacob, saying, 'To your *descendents I will give it.*' And I will send My Angel before you, and I will drive out the Canaanite and the Amorite and the Hittite and the Perizzite and the Hivite and the Jebusite. Go up to a land flowing with milk and honey; *for I will not go up in your midst*, lest I consume you on the way, for you are a stiff-necked people."
> —EXODUS 33:1–3, EMPHASIS ADDED

I thank God for sending His presence before us despite our shortcomings. God is so merciful, and all He wants from us is our obedience. I believe that I am at a place where I know my destiny. Not only do I know what I am called to do, but I also have an understanding of where God is leading me.

The challenge is obeying God at all cost. Remember what happened to Moses? He failed to obey God's instructions. God told Moses to speak to the rock so water could be retrieved for the people. Instead, Moses hit the rock twice, but the water still came out. So what's the problem? Moses failed to sanctify God in the eyes of the people with his disobedience.

It amazes me how leaders can be rebellious against God, but the water still comes out! Ministers often fall into the trap of sanctifying themselves in the eyes of the people instead of God. They give the people what they want, which in Moses' case was a show, but God received no glory.

God spoke to me this week and gave me a name for people who do such a thing—"glory-snatchers"! When ministers snatch His glory, it causes Christians to fall. Ezekiel 44:12–15 illustrates my point:

> "Because they ministered to them before their idols and caused the house of Israel to fall into iniquity, therefore I have raised My hand in an oath against them," says the Lord GOD, "that they shall bear their iniquity. And they shall not come near Me to minister to Me as priest, nor come near any of My holy things, nor into the Most Holy Place; but they shall bear their shame and their abominations which they have committed. Nevertheless I will make them keep charge of the temple, for all its work, and for all that has to be done in it. But the priests, the Levites, the sons of Zadok, who kept charge of My sanctuary when the children of Israel went astray from Me, they shall come near Me to minister to Me; and they shall stand before Me to offer to Me the fat and the blood," says the Lord GOD.

Moses accomplished the purpose of God for his life by bringing the people out of Egypt. But his accomplishment should have taken him into the Promised Land. It is a curse to see the promise but never taste it. The Bible says we should "taste and see that the LORD is good" (Ps. 34:8). Many believers are satisfied carrying Bibles around and quoting scriptures. I call them "Bible toters" and "Scripture quoters." Hebrews 4:2 warns us of people who hear the Word of God but do not benefit from it.

The passage goes on to say they forfeit their lot in life and do not enter God's rest. That's because they fail to appropriate properly the promises of God. Moses saw the hope of his purpose, but he did not enter his destiny.

My greatest fear is to bring others out of bondage and not be able to go "in" myself. I am not just called out of darkness; God promises that I can enter into His marvelous light. As ministers of the gospel, we must walk in the anointing of the Zadok priest.

THE ANOINTING OF ZADOK

The regular priests were sinners, but God didn't remove them from ministry. He proclaimed a greater curse on them. God said they could be in charge of the sanctuary, but He wouldn't allow them to come close to Him.

I am standing in the gap for those who desire to be Zadok priests. But the call is for those who want to do more than just come out of bondage. It's for those who want to enter their promised land and maintain the power to stay in God's presence.

Zadok priests have the ability to stand before God and offer the "fat" and the "blood." They have not sold out to the gods of fortune and destiny called Meni and Gad. The fat represents the finest part, but the blood represents innocence. The other priests could not come close to God, but in the end they would have to stand before Him in judgment.

> I BELIEVE THAT I AM AT A PLACE WHERE I KNOW MY DESTINY. NOT ONLY DO I KNOW WHAT I AM CALLED TO DO, BUT I ALSO HAVE AN UNDERSTANDING OF WHERE GOD IS LEADING ME.

God warned me that the giants in the promised land would not be like my wilderness challenges. Wilderness challenges were lack and need, but promised land giants are fortune and destiny. Read Isaiah 65:11 (AMP):

But you who forsake the Lord, who forget and ignore My holy Mount [Zion], who prepare a table for Gad [the Babylonian god of fortune] and who furnish mixed drinks for Meni [the god of destiny] . . .

All that I've come out of means nothing if I cannot stand before God at the end, prosperous and innocent. I have been delivered to my destiny, and I purpose not to flirt with the Babylonian gods of destiny and fortune!

Not only has God brought me into the prosperity of my destiny, but I am also covered with the blood of Jesus, and because of the blood I stand innocent today. I pray that as you read this book you too will be encouraged to keep your date with destiny.

CHAPTER 1

A DATE WITH DESTINY

I N 1988 I received a prophetic word that changed my life. A prophetess told me, "You will pastor in a neighborhood that has become a waste place. The church building will need a facelift, but God will supernaturally provide for the renovation." She went on to tell me how people would travel from around the nation to receive deliverance from spiritual bondage at the church.

As she explained how God would physically and spiritually restore the neighborhood near the ministry, my ears could not believe what I was hearing. My natural mind could not fathom a former drug abuser like me ministering on this level to anyone. As a result of the prophetic word, many have crossed the threshold of Spoken Word Ministries and have experienced the delivering power of Jesus Christ.

It seems like yesterday when Bishop Quan Miller and Wallace Sibley of the Church of God in Florida gave me the keys to the building located on the corner of Steele and Blue Street. The building was a historical sight for the national African American Church of God conventions. They held their national conventions at the church located on the corner of Steele and Blue. The Church of God built a better facility and moved to another part of town. Since that time, thriving in that neighborhood was difficult for any pastor who attempted to do so.

Bishop Miller, the state overseer at the time, didn't really know me. After he handed me the keys to the building on Wednesday, he instructed me to have the electricity turned on and have church on Sunday.

The church that was prophesied to me manifested before my eyes the first Sunday in January 1996.

It was just as the prophecy had revealed. It was large enough to comfortably seat nine hundred people, and the area was a haven for drug trafficking. This didn't faze me in the least. Inhabiting this tough neighborhood were my future ministers and preachers.

Before I even knew the building would be my church, God told me to ride around in my car and pray over the city. I was claiming the streets of Jacksonville, Florida, for Jesus. God told me to drive around a perimeter of the Durkeville area seven times. On the seventh lap around, He told me to shout the victory. Steele and Blue were in this area.

As I did, I quickly caught the attention of many of the drug dealers. I'm sure they thought I was on the down low, covertly helping the police bust dealers. I remember during my final trip around the block that day, I shouted at the top of my voice. All the people in the neighborhood looked at me like I was crazy, but I felt the walls come down!

A LEPER LEANS TOWARD THE TWILIGHT HOUR

With all of the obstacles that had come against us on Steele and Blue, it sometimes appeared as if the people were virtually unreachable. Women and men sold their bodies the way car salesmen sell used cars. They would transact business right on the steps of the church. Sometimes things seemed so hard, but giving up was never an option for me.

Though my circumstances were not exactly a pastor's delight, I could not forget from where God had brought me. I was so grateful God had called me to ministry that what seemed to be failure wasn't so bad! Many preachers tried to revive the church, but the neighborhood was a challenge. Cars were frequently stolen, and people feared for their lives as they entered and exited the building.

Some of the most hard-core, criminally minded people in the city lived near my church. But I wasn't unfamiliar to the area. These streets were my hangout when I was strung out on drugs. I remembered what it was like to have a criminal mind, so it made it easy for me to reach out to the residents.

I was in a neighborhood of lepers. In truth, I felt like a leper myself! This was not such a bad thing, because God reminded me of the four lepers who sat at the gates of Samaria. When a great famine fell on the land, everyone—the lepers included—thought they would surely die.

Trouble wasn't limited to my neighborhood, as in the case of Samaria; the entire city seemed to be in a hopeless situation. In fact, lepers always appear to be worse off because of their open wounds and sores. Everybody knows a leper is in trouble, but those who keep their wounds undercover go unnoticed. Jesus said it's the sick who need a physician. If people won't admit they need help, who will help them?

My city, Jacksonville, needed help, but we had no voice that would hit the streets and declare it. Jacksonville has powerful ministries that have touched nations, but at the time, a place people could run to for true deliverance was null and void. Unbelievers needed a place they could run to for salvation and safety.

At Spoken Word Ministries, we have church members who have had sex changes, participated in high-level occult rituals, witnessed shape-shifting (the changing of human beings into animals), and many other sinful problems. Please do not think of our church as

11

a place of horror or freaks. God has beautifully transformed these people.

Today, you can't detect who came out of what, because all things have become new! We also have business owners, professional athletes, Hollywood agents, and models who attend the church. There are many others society deemed unregenerate, but God sent His Son.

Sometimes you have to be a leper and become a reproach in the eyes of men to get the goods or the souls God has assigned to your care. The Book of Second Kings tells us that the lepers figured they could either continue to sit, do nothing, and wait for change to come to them, or they could go into the enemy's camp and take back the goods that were taken.

The hardest part of feeling like a leper was knowing what people thought of me. Regardless of what church people thought of me, I knew I had nothing to lose! People already thought the worst of me, so I might as well "bust a move!" Sometimes a person has no choice but to get up and do something, because nobody wants to help a leper.

The Bible says that when the lepers decided to get up and do something for themselves, God sent a delusion that caused the enemy to flee in fear.

The enemy loves it when we soak in self-pity. No matter how bad things get, if you don't help yourself, you're in trouble. When we get up from what is holding us down, it sends confusion to the enemy's camp.

The lepers gained victory by "getting up!" When they got up it was twilight—the same hour God gave them victory over their enemies. Like the leprous condition in biblical times, there was no provision in the city or in my church. I had no one to whom I could turn to make my vision come to pass. I was in an abusive marriage that resulted in a divorce, and my name as a minister became a reproach.

No one in the church community wanted to deal with me,

and those who supported me were lepers just like me. We were living day to day and week to week, but God always provided. I made the decision to go where the provision was—in the enemy's camp!

The great thing about the lepers mentioned in 2 Kings 7:3 is they delivered the goods to the city. Isn't it just like God to deliver provision through folk who were considered a reproach? When the lepers came back with the goods, people were no longer afraid of their disease.

The Bible never said the lepers were healed. It was as if their disease no longer mattered. People in the community didn't refuse the nourishment the lepers provided, because they were starving. We are spiritually starving in America, and God is birthing "leper ministries." Ministries that some people consider the least are willing to share the gospel with the multitudes.

> THE HARDEST PART OF FEELING LIKE A LEPER WAS KNOWING WHAT PEOPLE THOUGHT OF ME. REGARDLESS OF WHAT CHURCH PEOPLE THOUGHT OF ME, I KNEW I HAD NOTHING TO LOSE! PEOPLE ALREADY THOUGHT THE WORST OF ME, SO I MIGHT AS WELL "BUST A MOVE!"

In my city, we weren't experiencing a famine of food or water, but a "deliverance famine." There was a shortage of solid, ground-level, deliverance ministry. Somehow, the enemy crept in and slandered the ministry of warfare and deliverance. God moved for us miraculously, but the closer we got to our breakthrough, the darker it got. This is what happens before the twilight hour.

THE TWILIGHT HOUR

Twilight is the time when drastic change occurs. The Old Testament character Jacob wrestled with the angel all night, but his breakthrough came at the crack of dawn. Until he could see the light, he held on to God all night long. In the darkest hour, even the faintest crack of light seems wonderfully bright. Isaiah talks about the glory of Zion.

> Arise, and shine; for thy light is come, and the glory of the LORD is risen upon thee. For, behold, the darkness shall cover the earth, and gross darkness the people: but the LORD shall arise upon thee, and his glory shall be seen upon thee. And the Gentiles shall come to thy light, and kings to the brightness of thy rising.
>
> —ISAIAH 60:1–3, KJV

It's true that real brightness comes out of dark situations. The darker your situation, the greater you'll shine when you come out. The Book of Isaiah speaks of the Gentiles coming to our "light and the kings to the brightness of our rising." The world needs ministry that will make a difference in the lives of people right where they are. Sinners need leaders who understand darkness, who are not judgmental.

I believed the black cloud that lingered over my area of town was an indication of demonic activity in the community. The Bible says that where sin abounds (the devil is moving), grace does abound much more (God is moving).

Our church building was literally haunted. During intercessory prayer, giant ants and cockroaches attacked us like the plagues of pestilence. During worship services, the doors to the church would open and close without any human assistance.

As a constant reminder that we were in a spiritually dead neighborhood, the church had a stench we couldn't mask. But at Spoken Word, we were willing to pay the price even as the enemy came at us from every direction with attempts to shut us down. In facing each challenge, I often think about the prophetic words spoken over my life.

As a church, we withstood the storms during our early days in ministry. By His grace, we escaped the snares of Lilith—the desert monster mentioned in the Book of Isaiah. The monster was an avowed enemy of newborn babies and swore to kill them before they turned a year old. We were also very successful in breaking the power of crib death over our church.

I believe Lilith is the spirit that is dispatched to snuff out newborn churches. The first year of a church's existence is as delicate as the first year of a newborn baby's life. Spiritual crib death must be bound and severely dealt with. A similar demon, Lamia, is a vampire spirit that aids women in abortion or forces them to miscarry. This spirit attacks churches and causes them to abort their vision.

The demonic attacks we experienced were bad, but the plight of our membership was getting worse. For two years we could count the number of visitors we had on one hand, and even on Easter Sunday there were no new faces. At the time, we had four families in our church, which totaled eighteen people. That was including children and teenagers. After my divorce, I remarried a former drug dealer after he gave his life to Christ. His name is Ardell, but we call him Danny. My marriage made me even less popular among the church community.

In the midst of our difficulties, we saw a slither of light. The light had finally come. We began to experience breakthrough after breakthrough. After years of sitting alone, God began to confirm our ministry.

We went into the Assyrian camp to take back what the enemy had stolen from us, and the spoils were plenty! God began to save and deliver those who were considered untouchables. We saw signs, wonders, and miracles on a daily basis. Both my father and stepfather accepted Christ as Lord, and close family members joined the church.

DEMONIC PROPHECY

Just as God sent prophetic words about my destiny, Satan sent lies and threats to me. One day a man called me from a local cult group he called Eifi. He explained that he was studying to become a voodoo priest. I later found out the group he belonged to was known as the Yoruba religion. Yoruba's foundation is rooted in ancestry worship.

The anonymous caller explained that he had been sending death curses to my demon-buster buddy, Evangelist Mona, and me. It was Evangelist Mona who prophesied Spoken Word Ministries would come out of my belly. She named us Demon Busters and was the first one I heard yell, "Hey ho, devil, you gotta go!"

I could never quite say those words like Evangelist Mona. When she would preach the gospel, the gates of hell trembled. Many were baffled about her early death, though. I knew what was going on!

The caller said his powers were not working against us and that he had concluded we must be on the right track. Before he hung up the telephone, he told me how he wanted to leave the craft if he could find a sure way out. He also said very strongly to me, "Whatever you are doing, keep on doing it!" The words of that warlock never left my mind. I didn't write him off as a crazy person though the words he spoke made no sense.

Many young musicians have tapped into Yoruba to conjure up spirits of popular singers who have died. India.Arie, Erykah Badu, and other popular singers pay homage to their spirit guides during public events. The following quote was taken from a prominent entertainment magazine:

> D'Angelo recorded his long-awaited new album, *Voodoo* (Virgin), at Electric Lady Studio, which Jimi Hendrix built on Eighth Street in Manhattan's Greenwich Village. The studio pet, a white cat named Jimi, would follow D'Angelo around and curl up in his lap while D' worked out some lyric or chord. And of course, he has nightmares about

16

conjuring up Marvin Gaye. He was channeling the dirty mind the artist abandoned for Jehovah.

But *Voodoo* isn't about them. It is about grandmother and grandfather and tambourines. And the tarrying that goes on till four in the morning because sometimes it's slow coming, baring one's soul. Becoming naked to God, vulnerable to the ancestors and their ancient tongues. Sometimes it takes three whole years of tarrying to call a spirit down.*

The above statement refers to a popular pop artist today. The magazine cover refers to him as "casting soulful spells," and he is said to have blessed the public with his otherworldly album *Voodoo*. The article credits the inspiration behind his music to growing up in the church, the birth of his son, and channeling souls.

Yoruba is becoming a fad to the old and young, rich and the poor. Mixing voodoo and Catholicism draws those who have no sense of belonging and those who seek to be a part of something they feel is powerful. The temporary benefits, however, are a one-way route to death.

A Casualty of War

As I think back on the phone call from the Eifi priest, it almost seems unreal. The only thing that testifies of its reality is Evangelist Mona's untimely death from a rare disease. Though we casually kept in contact, the enemy had slowly severed my relationship with her.

After her death, I found out my friend had done so many terrible things against me. When God restored my relationship with pastors in the city, many of them came to me and repented of turning against me because of the things Evangelist Mona had told them.

She was dead, and there was no way for me to figure out what happened to our relationship. It is a strange thing to think you have a close friend and then find out she is not for you.

Despite the circumstances, I will always love and respect her. I will never forget the fun we had in the worst parts of town while winning souls for the Lord and setting the captives free. The church community was devastated by her death. Evangelist Mona was loved by many, and all she talked about was Jesus.

The problem was she didn't heed the warning of the Eifi priest, and she stopped doing what kept her alive—spiritual warfare! My demon-busting buddy and dear sister in the Lord had gone home early. I believe there are many pastors in my city who have died early due to witchcraft. We must fight the good fight of faith, but faith without works is dead.

God has given us power over all the powers of the enemy, but if we can't use it wisely, the price of our decision is grave.

As I write this book, I am the same age Evangelist Mona was at the time of her death. I thank God for abundant life and the power He has given us over darkness. Evangelist Mona's death was one of the hardest things I had ever dealt with, because I believe she died as a result of spiritual warfare.

> GOD HAS GIVEN US POWER OVER ALL THE POWERS OF THE ENEMY, BUT IF WE CAN'T USE IT WISELY, THE PRICE OF OUR DECISION IS GRAVE.

She had stopped doing deliverance on the level that we began. I plan to obey God all the days of my life and live a long life. She had become a casualty of war.

I had a dream about Evangelist Mona six months before her death. In the dream, we were preaching at an outdoor meeting, and I was to speak first. I began to address some demons very radically.

After I finished talking, I passed the microphone to Evangelist Mona. She quietly smiled and laid the microphone down. She looked at me and said, "I don't want to be involved." At that point she turned and boarded a helicopter that disappeared into the sky.

I did not have an understanding of the dream at the time, but it made me feel incredibly sad. A few months after the dream, I visited with Evangelist Mona in a beauty salon. She never mentioned she was sick, nor did she ask me to pray for her.

We talked about going on the road and ministering together again. I was so excited to spend time with her that I never noticed the frailness of her body under the apron she wore.

Not long after that day, I received a call to go and pray for Evangelist Mona, because she was dying. I could not believe my ears. Within thirty minutes of that call, as I stood by the phone allowing the reality of the words I had just heard to sink in, Evangelist Mona was dead! I never got a chance to pray for her. How could two people who were once so close grow so far apart?

I know I have at least one witness in heaven. As I write this book, my thoughts are often of her. She was an important part of my foundation in the Lord. Her godly lifestyle and instruction laid a blueprint in my life that is now reaching nations. One day we will fellowship again in heaven.

I miss Evangelist Mona dearly, but for now I must continue my course. I must be honest and say that Evangelist Mona had begun to get caught up in the program of the church and forgot the purpose of the church. When Evangelist Mona laid down the microphone in my dream and said she didn't want to get involved, I knew she had lost her radical edge.

No matter what arises, I have to keep doing what I have been called to do. I realize that it may cost me relationships, family, and friends, but I must press toward the mark. As for me, I am called to cast out devils and manifest the glory of God in the earth realm. I will not settle for anything less!

Vibe, April 2000.

CHAPTER 2

UPTOWN GIRL

ON JUNE 12, 1961, I was born in Jacksonville, Florida, in an area known to the local blacks as "uptown." (Most people called it "downtown," but to us it was "uptown.")

My grandfather, grandmother, mother, Aunt Maude, my two younger sisters, Thabathia and Sebrena, and I all lived together in a wooden house. When the city condemned our home, we moved a few doors down to a big apartment with a bar located below.

Growing up, I did not spend a lot of time with my mother, because she worked a lot. She was attractive, tall, and had big, pretty eyes. Everyone said that she looked like a model. Everybody in our house worked except my blind grandmother. She stayed at home, and I got to stay home and help her. No one ever called my real mother "Momma," we just called her by her nickname, Bobbie, because my grandmother was "Momma" or "Big Momma."

My grandmother gave birth to three daughters: my mom, Lillie

Mae, and Maude. Lillie Mae was the oldest, and Maude was the youngest. My mom was the middle child. Maude was very smart in school and went to college to become a nurse.

My aunts told me stories about my family that fascinated me. My grandmother met my grandfather, Charlie Walter Parrish (or "Mr. Bubba"), in Raiford Prison on the chain gang. My grandfather did all kinds of illegal things, and my grandmother was incarcerated for murder. According to Lillie Mae, my mother was conceived at Raiford.

Though Lillie Mae did not live with us, she always came to the rescue when havoc upset our household. Out of everyone in my household, my grandfather and grandmother played the major roles in the lives of my two sisters and me.

LIFE WITH MISS ELLA MAE

My grandmother was the authoritarian in the house, even though she had no eyes. She was not born blind but at one time had twenty-twenty vision. My grandmother had an extensive history with the police department for fighting, and she never fought unarmed. She and my grandfather came from a small town called Madison, Florida, about fifty miles outside of Tallahassee. They moved to Jacksonville, because they were barred from Madison County for causing trouble. Her married name was Mrs. Ella Mae Parrish, but she was a Taylor by birth. Everyone who knew her well called her Big Momma.

My grandmother was said to be some kind of tough woman. Even in a time when blacks were expected to be soft-spoken toward white people, she was loud and boisterous. One day I remember watching her pull her underwear down and flash her backside to a policeman.

I was privileged to meet the officer that Big Momma flashed before he died. He told me how he would ride her around for hours, allow her to drink in the back of the police car until she fell out, and then take her back home. The police frequented our residence so much that many of the officers tried to work with my unruly, blind grandmother.

My grandmother was a very large, big-breasted woman. She carried all kinds of things in the center of her bra, which she called her "bosom." My grandmother stuffed her bosom with guns, knives, liquor bottles, and even her peach snuff.

Over and over again, I would ask Aunt Lillie Mae to recount how Big Momma became blind. One of Big Momma's eye sockets had no eyeball and was closed shut, and the other eyeball was a grayish, pale color.

According to Lillie Mae, Big Momma had a white boyfriend who was obsessed with her. He had purchased a refrigerator for her, and they had a discrepancy over it. When they started fighting, the man picked up an ax and hit Big Momma across the forehead. Her skull was cracked, and she was left blind in the left eye. Big Momma had to get a metal plate in her head because of that fight. In response to this incident, she shot her boyfriend seven times and went to the Raiford chain gang.

> MY GRANDMOTHER WAS SAID TO BE SOME KIND OF TOUGH WOMAN. EVEN IN A TIME WHEN BLACKS WERE EXPECTED TO BE SOFT-SPOKEN TOWARD WHITE PEOPLE, SHE WAS LOUD AND BOISTEROUS.

Lillie Mae said my grandmother lost her other eye during a fight with my grandfather. She was swinging an ice pick at him when she fell off of the porch. As she lost her balance, she lost her grip on the ice pick, and it plucked out her right eyeball. Based on the story, the eyeball was hanging from the cord that connected it to the socket while it lay on her chest.

In a fit of rage, she attempted to pull the eyeball by the cord completely out of her head and cursed at God, telling Him that He might as well take both of her eyes.

UNDERSTANDING MY GRANDMA

Even though my grandma loved us, she had a strange way of showing it. She would curse me like a sailor and hug me at the same time. No one physically disciplined us except her. And because of my grandmother's handicap, I was her eyes and hands. I saw and did what she could not see and do. She drank Smirnoff Vodka, dipped peach snuff, used Noxzema skin cream, drank the short-bottled Coca-Cola, and chewed Juicy Fruit gum. Whenever she needed something, I was the one she called to get it.

I will never forget her spit can, an empty coffee can that she spit her snuff into. Often she would kick it over or drop it, and guess who had to clean it up! It was the most disgusting sight.

My grandmother was blind, but she wasn't stupid. She would constantly accuse my grandfather of having affairs with other women. And whenever she thought she was certain of his indiscretions, she would torture the *other* woman.

I remember one time when she made me lead her up to one of those ladies in a bar. We were living in the apartment house over the bar at the time. Grandmother briefed me on how to lead her up to the lady and then back away. Though I was crying on the inside, I dared not let a peep or whimper escape.

As my grandmother walked up to the lady, she pulled a switch-blade from her bra and put it to the lady's throat. Though she threatened the woman, she did not kill her. It must not have been that lady's day to die, because it surely was within my grandmother's capacity to kill her.

My aunt Lillie Mae told me that my grandfather went to the emergency room many nights because of my grandmother's attempts on his life. I will never forget the time she made me lead her up to him, and she slit his chest wide open. I remember the blood spurting onto my face. I was only six years old at the time.

Can you imagine how traumatic that was for a six-year-old? My grandmother's decision to use me to do her dirty work left a horrible mark on my life, which you will read about in later chapters.

My grandmother always talked about Jesus, but I never remember a day that she went to church. She did religiously believe in her psychic dream book, though. How could a blind woman read a dream book without Braille? Easily—

> MOST GIRLS MOLESTED AT A YOUNG AGE EXPERIENCE ABUSE AFTER ABUSE AS THEY GET OLDER, BECAUSE IT IS A VICIOUS CYCLE.

through her five-year-old granddaughter, me! I learned to read with understanding at the age of five by reading my grandmother's psychic dream book.

The early years in a child's life are so important. It is the time when children are molded into what they will become in the future. A consistent, positive, and secure home life can prepare a child for his or her divine destiny. But despite the sinful influences of childhood, by the blood of Jesus and His delivering power, negative forces that come against children in the early years can be wiped out.

SHAME IN THE FAMILY

My most horrible experience as a child living with my grandmother happened when I was three years old. An eight-year-old boy, Tito, and I were playing in a small room in the back of the house that we called the "back porch." The little boy tried to sexually molest me. My cousin walked in and saw what was happening. My young

25

mind had no idea that what he was doing to me was wrong. My cousin yelled at the top of her voice, alerting Big Momma.

I will never forget Big Momma's response: "Bring that little whore to me! She ain't going to be nothing but a whore like her momma!" I didn't even know what a whore was, but judging from her tone, I knew it was something bad.

My family was too ignorant to realize I was being molested. Though this boy never physically penetrated my body, the devil wanted to penetrate my mind with the memory. Most girls molested at a young age experience abuse after abuse as they get older, because it is a vicious cycle. I was nearly scathed by another arrow of abuse in the same year by one of Tito's brothers, Reginald, who was a grown man.

> I LOVED MY GRANDDADDY SO MUCH. IF ANYBODY COULD PUT A SMILE ON MY FACE, HE COULD. HE WAS THE ONE WHO HUGGED US AND SPENT TIME WITH US.

Reginald was babysitting me while my mother ran to the store. He sat me on his lap and began to gyrate his body against mine. After the first incident on the back porch, something in me knew this was not right. He only tried it for a few seconds, but it seemed forever.

My mom came back quickly, but I was afraid to tell anyone what I had experienced. By God's mercy, I was never touched by another man during my childhood. As I grew older my cousin would point her finger at me about what happened on the "back porch." I hated to be reminded of this dirty memory, but I refused to believe it was my fault.

When I was around thirty years old, I ran into Reginald uptown. I hadn't seen him since I was a child. I pulled him to the side and told him that I remembered what he had done to me when I was a little girl. I tried to lead him to the Lord, but he walked away from me looking puzzled.

Not too long ago, I ran into Reginald's and Tito's other brother, James. James was walking down the street coming back from Reginald's funeral. He explained that Reginald had been suffering from an illness for many years. He died in a wheelchair with both of his legs cut off. Tito, the one who tried to molest me, also died a cruel, tormenting death through disease.

Thank God for My Granddaddy

My grandfather, Charlie Walter Parrish, was called Mr. Bubba in the neighborhood, but on his job he was called Mr. Charlie. Though I spent countless hours with Big Momma, the closest bond we experienced as children was with our granddaddy. I loved my granddaddy so much. If anybody could put a smile on my face, he could. He was the one who hugged us and spent time with us. And when everybody was working, partying, fussing, or just too busy, he always spent time with his granddaughters. He cooked dinner every night after he came home from work. To me, my grandfather was mother and father in one package.

Every Friday was payday, and when my granddaddy stepped off the city bus, it was always with a big box of goodies. The one treat I particularly remember him bringing us was Cracker Jacks.

We called my granddaddy "Daddy." Even though he was an alcoholic for many years, he would not sip a drink until he was sure we were bathed, fed, and ready for bed. He drank Fleischmann's Gin with no chaser. A fifth of liquor would last him a night. He would drink and smoke his Camel cigarettes until he passed out, and we would laugh and play tricks on him when he had reached his limit.

I can still picture Daddy, sitting in a chair with mucus running from his nose, his head nodding up and down like a heroine addict. We would hide under the bed or in the closet and yell to scare him. He would curse us out and try to run after us. He rarely spanked us, but when he did, we laughed while he tried to do it. Although people might say we had a very dysfunctional family situation, I am grateful for the ways my granddaddy made our house something of a home.

My grandfather's untimely and horrible death was one of the hardest things I have ever had to deal with in my life. While I was training for the Olympic trials, my grandfather was murdered uptown. This was too much for me to bear. He was robbed and his room set on fire. I was not saved at the time, so I flew home to look for the one who had killed my only true daddy. Word on the street was that a mentally retarded woman he was dating robbed him.

> TO ME, MY GRANDFATHER WAS MOTHER AND FATHER IN ONE PACKAGE.

THE ROOTS OF MRS. ELLA MAE PARRISH

When I wrote *Against All Odds*, there were so many things I did not know. The main thing I have recently learned is that my grandmother was a real witch. When you got to know her, she was a loving woman behind the scenes, but to an enemy she was a terror! She knew how to walk on the dark side of the supernatural.

It was so hard for me to understand as a young child, but it is all coming together now. My grandmother would brag about her powers to her daughters. My aunt said Big Momma would go to the homes of her enemies to speak curses on them. As part of the curse, she would shake dust on their doorways to get the results she wanted. I was told she and my grandfather were released from prison by means of witchcraft. My aunt said Big Momma would visit a white man who gave her spiritual advice.

In regards to my grandfather, he had been on the chain gang for three different crimes before he met my grandmother. He was first convicted as a teenager. But my aunt said he wasn't always guilty. She said that, as a black person, if you made the wrong white person mad, you could easily be sent to prison. Granddaddy did not start teenage life as a criminal, but his bouts with "the white man" changed his heart.

What began as a roadblock to destiny became a permanent detour. My grandfather was a convict due to racial prejudice and abuse. The white man my grandmother would visit to get spiritual advice told her to go to the jailhouse and visit my grandfather four times but never speak to him. She was instructed to only blow cigarette smoke in his face and leave.

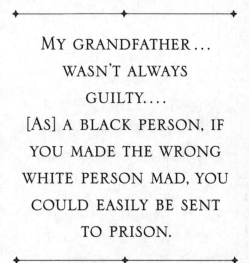

MY GRANDFATHER... WASN'T ALWAYS GUILTY.... [AS] A BLACK PERSON, IF YOU MADE THE WRONG WHITE PERSON MAD, YOU COULD EASILY BE SENT TO PRISON.

My grandfather was cursing her out, calling her all kinds of names, because he thought she had lost her mind. He did not understand why she would come to visit him and never say a word. She finally explained that she had to "fix" some things. She told Granddaddy not to worry and that he would be out soon. She also told him that the white man who initiated the warrant would not show up for court. The man never showed up, and my grandfather was released. Witchcraft is real!

My aunt Maude recently told me that my grandmother believed she was blind because God was punishing her for all the evil she had done. My aunt said Big Momma would always say she had to "pay her dues."

I finally found out what all of this meant. My grandmother was saved when she was twelve years old. Aunt Lillie Mae said my grandmother backslid and would literally curse God at times. And by this time in her life, she knew the Scriptures like the back of her hand. I would often wonder how she could sit in her chair drunk and quote verses about the End Times.

GRANDMA CHUNKIE

Mrs. Ella Mae's mother, Mary Jones Taylor, lived in Madison, Florida. She was a strong Christian woman, but for some reason I had never heard of her. She died before I was born.

She was the wife of Simeon Taylor, who was one of the few black men in his county who had his own farm. He had tobacco fields, cotton fields, and a lot of livestock. No one ever heard his wife, Grandma Chunkie, use profanity. This was unheard of in our family, because everybody "cussed"!

Grandma Chunkie was a pretty woman, but like her blind daughter, she was a big woman. She knew God and was a powerful prayer warrior. I thank Jesus for the prayers of Grandma Chunkie! But how could Grandma Chunkie have a daughter like Ella Mae Parrish? And just to think, I thought I just popped up saved out of nowhere. God always has a righteous remnant, and He is forever moving behind the scenes.

> GRANDMA CHUNKIE WAS A PRETTY WOMAN, BUT LIKE HER BLIND DAUGHTER, SHE WAS A BIG WOMAN. SHE KNEW GOD AND WAS A POWERFUL PRAYER WARRIOR. I THANK JESUS FOR THE PRAYERS OF GRANDMA CHUNKIE!

Relatives that I had no idea existed contacted me after the first edition of *Against All Odds* was published. They sent me a family tree that said my paternal great-great-grandfather was a full-blooded Cherokee Indian. I am a part of the fifth generation in his bloodline.

I have always known the Parrish family, but God has recently introduced me to the Hardy family. Many of my family members on the Hardy side are born-again believers. Wouldn't it be just like the devil to keep me away from them!

CHAPTER 3

UPTOWN ROOTS

UPTOWN, WHERE WE grew up, was a tough place. I learned early that when you were uptown, anything could happen. The rule pertaining to uptown was that either you "beat up" or you *got* "beat up." You had to earn a reputation on the streets in order to avoid constant harassment.

When it came to fighting, my grandmother did not play around. She instructed us to be the same way. If we were confronted, our instructions from her were not to come home until we kicked the life out of someone. Big Momma also told us that if one of us fought, *all* of us had to fight. So if one got dirty in a scuffle, we all rolled in the dirt to pass her test when we got home.

A BREAK-IN GONE BAD

Even when we were at home, our lives weren't safe from the street dangers. I will never forget the time a man broke into my aunt's house through a window in the back of the house and put a knife to her neck to rape her. My mother was bathing my two sisters and me as we sang a song she had taught us. My mom was on the go a lot, so those moments when we sang together really stick in my mind. But this time our joy was interrupted by a terrible scream by my aunt Maude: "Momma, there is a man in the house!"

We lived in what was called a "shotgun house." It had a long, narrow hall, and my grandmother always sat on the side of the hall entrance, where she slept. She rarely slept in a bed. That night, after my aunt screamed, the man frantically ran down the hall toward my grandmother. I guess he was trying to get away before someone called the police. Unfortunately for him, he had to pass by Big Momma.

As I mentioned earlier, Big Momma always kept a switchblade in her bra. Though she was blind, her senses were keen. She timed the steps of the running assailant's approach perfectly. As he passed her, she grabbed his shirt with one hand and began stabbing him with her other hand. Blood splattered everywhere.

I peered around the corner, and my eyes took in the entire scene. My grandmother was literally growling and cursing this man as she stabbed him over and over again. She had a death grip on him that he could not loosen.

As I looked at my grandmother's face, it appeared as if she relished every wound she inflicted on him. As for the man, he looked as if he was about to go into shock. When he finally broke away, he tore the front screen from our door while making his getaway. That night he came through the wrong window!

GROWING UP FAST AND FATHERLESS

Looking back, it seems like I always needed to grow up faster to keep up with everything my grandmother and my neighborhood required of me. Yes, there were other adults around, but somehow it always seemed like it was just the two of us—Big Momma and me.

My grandfather, likewise, was truly my daddy, because my two sisters and I each had different natural fathers, and none of them were around much. Of our three fathers, mine was seen the most, because he tended to his various businesses, legal and illegal, just around the corner from where we lived.

My father was into the numbers game. My grandmother ran the bolida, which is an illegal version of lotto. She often sent me to Ms. Tibby's house to deliver numbers and money. My grandmother and Ms. Tibby had a lot in common: their Coca-Colas, the BC and Stanback powders they took for headaches, and the respect they got from the streets.

My natural father, Andrew Preston Perkins, was a highly respected man in the black community. Everybody called him Perk. He was a very handsome man and was known for having nice-looking women. When I told people that I was Perk's daughter, they would respond by asking me, "Who was your momma?"

Perk was not a man who joked around a lot, and he did not take orders easily from anybody. During the sixties, my father started a group called the "Boomerang Gang." Many blacks in the Jacksonville area were proud of this radical group, because they stood against segregation laws.

At the time, there were two blacks on the local city council, and my father and his gang would escort them to work. Both blacks and whites were afraid, because no one knew what to expect.

There were many race riots that consisted of fistfights and even armed conflict. Radical black activists made plans to burn down white businesses in the downtown area, blocks away from uptown. My father and leaders of the Boomerang Gang were awarded at a big ceremony for calming the black community and opening doors for reconciliation.

For the first thirteen years of my life, Perk never publicly claimed me as his daughter. I often visited him at the bar. Everyone knew I looked like he spit me out, but it just was not a conversation piece. I remember when my daddy was running for a seat on the city council. One of the homosexuals that worked at the bar came to my house. He was going back and forth with my mom about why they should take me to the campaign party. I could hear our homosexual friend saying, "Now you know that baby needs to be with her daddy in his time of glory."

My grandmother yelled, "She ain't going!" As a child I could not understand why I could not be with my dad during his campaign activity. As I grew older I understood that an illegitimate child was not good for any campaign. Despite this, seeing poster boards of my dad, his wife, and other children around the city did not make it easy.

My mother showed no motive for proving that I was Perk's child. But when people looked at my pecan tan complexion and my extremely curly hair I inherited from my daddy,

◆————————◆————————◆

MY FATHER AND LEADERS OF THE BOOMERANG GANG WERE AWARDED AT A BIG CEREMONY FOR CALMING THE BLACK COMMUNITY AND OPENING DOORS FOR RECONCILIATION.

◆————————◆————————◆

they knew the deal. My mother never seemed to be in love with my dad; it was as if I was something that just happened between them. From the time I was born until this day, they have been friends. They have never had a dispute, and my mom never pursued child support.

My father's mother, Grandma Perkins, always sent me money and nice gifts. She was the most beautiful woman I had ever seen. When I was a child, her hair looked to me like a white person's hair. It was straight and coal black; it flowed down her back. She had several businesses, which was unusual for a black woman in the 1960s. She turned over some of those businesses to my dad, who was her only son.

This is how Perk got his start. Grandma Perkins never denied I was her grandchild, even though Perk's name was not on my birth certificate. My mother had a boyfriend who really loved her. When she got pregnant with me, he asked her to let him make her name good by marrying him.

His name was Roosevelt, and he drove liquor trucks long distance. A few weeks after my mom decided she would marry him, his truck jackknifed, exploded, and he was tragically killed. I was too young to remember the incident, but my mom eventually told me after I recognized his name on my birth certificate.

My mom told me that after Roosevelt's death, she was determined to make it on her own. She had to do so not just for me but also for my sisters. Actually, as I look back, despite all the difficulty, I think my mom did a great job. My other sisters have successful lives today. Thabathia will retire from the post office soon, and Sebrena has over fifteen years on the police force. Both of them are members of my church.

FINALLY, ACCEPTANCE!

My father got my mother pregnant while he was married to a beautiful, fair-skinned woman named Cleo. Cleo and my dad often had public fights. She was a very outspoken woman. No matter what, Perk would never confess to her that he was the father of Mrs. Ella Mae's granddaughter. In fact, I will never forget when Cleo found out I was Perk's daughter.

She lived in a big house a few neighborhoods away from where I lived. A friend told me where Cleo lived with my oldest sister, Shawna. At that time I wasn't sure why I wanted to go to Cleo's house, but I went. Today, I know why I braved a possible altercation with her to knock on her door. I did it, because I wanted to see my brothers and sisters. My heart was beating fast as I stood and knocked. I had heard rumors that Cleo was something to deal with, and I did not know if she would curse me out.

Cleo opened the door, and I never had to say one word. She just started cursing at Perk. She called him a lying, no good, so-and-so. She looked at me and told me to come on in. "You are Perk's child. You look just like him! You look just like my baby boy!" That greeting was the beginning of a new friendship. To this day, Cleo has been wonderful to me.

Cleo is a very straightforward person. When I was seventeen, if I wanted to stay out all night, all I had to do was my housework. Today, I specialize in home-cooked meals and clean the house very well because of what Cleo taught me. Every Thanksgiving when I cook my meals, I call her to brush up on my down-South recipes. Cleo has had a great influence on my life, though her approach was negative. The bottom line is she instilled in me to be the best at whatever I did.

I will never forget her words: "If you going to be a ho, be a clean ho, be a good ho; don't ever be a dumb ho or a broke ho!" On Wednesdays, I had to work especially hard at Cleo's house. This was our weekly clean-up day. At night I went to the sissy shows. When my friends would call on Wednesday, Cleo would laugh and tell them, "Baby Kim is hanging out with her sissies!"

MY SISSIES

As a young girl I was drawn to the bar scene, because I loved the atmosphere. The bar featured "sissy shows" several times a week. We called them sissy shows because men would dress in drag and impersonate famous female singers. The term "sissy" did not offend them because it was part of our everyday language.

I loved the homosexual men at my daddy's bar and affectionately called them "my sissies." The most fascinating thing to me about "my sissies" was that after the show was over, these men continued to live as if they were women.

The apartment building I lived in over the bar was one floor above an apartment where a lot of homosexuals and transvestites lived. I believe my exposure to them as a child prepared me to minister to homosexuals today. I spent a lot of time with them, and to me they were just "regular people." There was a special place in my heart for them.

I have never been a lesbian, but I was raised in an environment with a strong homosexual influence. The uptown sissies seemed to, in their own way, have a level of respect. The atmosphere was ignited when they put on their shows. Straight and gay people alike would come from around the city to see them perform.

I can still hear the announcer, "And now, the Betty Moore Review!" My heart would beat fast, because one thing I could be sure of was that I would be entertained. Even though we never left Jacksonville, Florida, those singers took us to Broadway, the Apollo, and Hollywood.

They would impersonate singers such as Diana Ross, Patti LaBelle, and Tina Turner. I would bring my straight friends to the bar to show them what I thought "real life" was all about. As I got older, kids my age were busy trying to get dates to the prom or catch a ride to a house party, but not me; I was trying to get to the next sissy show.

As a child, I never questioned their lifestyle, because what they did was a part of my world. I loved my sissies, and ministering to homosexuals will forever be close to my heart! Today, I am proud to have an open door policy for people who want to be delivered from homosexuality—and for good reason. One Wednesday evening during Bible study, God blew my mind. I was preaching the Word of God and everything seemed normal until I looked in the back of the room. I could not believe my eyes. I saw one of "my sissies" sitting on a back pew. I was encouraged to preach harder. It was for no particular reason other than the joy of the Lord rising inside of me.

It was a powerful service, but I could not wait to meet my friend after the service was over. Billy looked just like a middle-aged woman. Only a few of my friends from the streets knew he was a man. He had a complete sex change and had been living as a woman for many years.

As I walked toward him he declared, "It is over!" I didn't know what he was talking about, but he said it again, "It is over! God has done it!" Billy was not the kind of homosexual you could just joke around with in the street if you didn't know him personally.

No one could call him a man and get away with it. He didn't play in the streets. He meant business! When I addressed him, I wasn't sure how to greet him without offending him. He explained that God had given him a miracle and that he wanted to give his testimony. I told him to come to church the following Sunday, and I would let him testify. I alerted security and told them to let him sit on the front row when he arrived for service.

> I LOVED MY SISSIES, AND MINISTERING TO HOMOSEXUALS WILL FOREVER BE CLOSE TO MY HEART! TODAY, I AM PROUD TO HAVE AN OPEN DOOR POLICY FOR PEOPLE WHO WANT TO BE DELIVERED FROM HOMOSEXUALITY.

I took extreme care in not offending Billy. I told security, "This is my people; when he comes Sunday please escort him to the front row." "My people" is slang on the streets to let someone know a person is all right to deal with.

On Sunday morning I was coming in from the Charisma Women's Conference, and my body was really tired. I was willing to let God use my tired body, but He had another plan. Billy was sitting on the front row when I arrived. The praise and worship was powerful, and we could tell God wanted to do something different, but what was it?

I turned the microphone over to Billy to give a quick testimony, and the power of God fell. As I looked into his eyes, all I could see was Jesus. His body looked like a woman, but I saw Jesus. Please don't attempt to figure out what was happening with your carnal mind, because you can't discern in the natural what I am trying to say.

Billy shared his testimony about how God had delivered him from a major stroke. He worked at the hospital and had a stroke while he was on duty. He was transported to the intensive care unit with his mind boggled about what was happening to his body. The stroke affected his sight and totally impaired the right side of his body. He described how the devil manifested at his hospital window and told him he was taking him out.

When Billy screamed the name of Jesus, he heard a demonic growl. God supernaturally healed Billy and left the doctors baffled. It was so miraculous that within a few days Billy was released to go home without physical therapy.

As Billy gave his testimony in my church that day, no one knew that he was a man. The cover was removed when he made a profound statement. He explained that his sister was taking him home from the hospital after he had his stroke. She was crying over what had happened to him. Billy told the church that he told his sister, "Do not feel sorry for me; God has given your brother another chance!"

I fell prostrate on the floor as I heard these words. I knew the significance of his testimony. A man who was *convinced* he was born a woman was now *admitting* he was a man. The church went crazy! The testimony of Billy's total recovery from a massive stroke was not the highlight of the story. Billy shared that he was seeking God after he returned home from the hospital. He was still partially blind but could get around on his own. The Holy Spirit kept telling him to go to a specific corner on his front porch.

BILLY'S OUT-OF-BODY EXPERIENCE

It was about 3:00 a.m., and Billy finally obeyed God. He began to pray his normal religious prayers when God quickened him to get real. Billy began to lay it all down and tell God everything. Suddenly, he was taken into the spirit realm. The first place he went was a neighborhood where I had a center for girls on drugs.

The neighborhood had large, old-fashioned houses that were used for all kinds of illegal activity. The area was also home to a large homosexual community in our city. When the Spirit of God took Billy to this neighborhood the houses were all destroyed. Billy asked God what this meant, and God told him he had nothing to go back to. God allowed Billy to see that even if he wanted to go back to his old lifestyle, he couldn't, because it had been destroyed.

Billy had quite a journey that day when God allowed him to go into the supernatural. But his trips to heaven and hell were the most amazing parts. The way Billy described heaven convinced everyone in the church he had been there. He spoke of the crystal river and described the road to heaven and the gate of heaven.

He said the road to heaven was so straight and shiny that it looked like a sword. And yes, God took him to hell, too. Billy said the road to hell was shaped like a snake. He talked about an ugly bridge that led into the entrance of hell and how it was engulfed with a dark, dreary cloud of smoke.

The thing that I remembered the most was when Billy said it was so dark in hell that it seemed like he had a black coat over his body. Billy began to cry out to God in repentance while he was in hell. He begged God to give him another chance. For the first time in his homosexual life, he knew without a doubt he was born to be a man, but he had to be taken to hell to receive this revelation.

How many lesbians are there in hell who have finally realized they were born to be women? How many homosexual men will have to go to hell before they get a revelation of their true identity? Billy is so special to my heart. He has shared with me that seven of his close friends have died from AIDS since his deliverance.

Before he underwent a sex change, he traveled with one of the largest gospel singers in America. Billy was raised in the church on the gospel music circuit. He said the perversion was so great that he ran from the church and decided to serve the devil all the way instead of playing with God, which is why he had a sex change operation.

Billy and I spent hours at my home sharing our uptown experiences and talking about the goodness of Jesus. Even though God has supernaturally spared him from the death sentence of AIDS, he is physically living as a eunuch.

The Bible says some eunuchs are born from the womb, men make some, and God ordains some.

> For there are eunuchs who have been born incapable of marriage; and there are eunuchs who have been made so by men; and there are eunuchs who have made themselves incapable of marriage for the sake of the kingdom of heaven. Let him who is able to accept this accept it.
> —MATTHEW 19:12, AMP

SHARING THE GOOD NEWS

There are two Greek translations for the word *eunuch: eunouchizo* and *eunouchos*. They both refer to an impotent or unmarried man. *Eunuch* also refers to a man that has been castrated. Billy shared with me that he had been impotent from birth. I do not believe homosexuals are born gay. On the other hand, after much prayer and searching the Scriptures, I can confirm that many are born eunuchs and believe they are gay.

Many hermaphrodites fall into the confusion of this type of

deception. Hermaphrodites are babies born with both male and female genitals. The fact is, they are either male or female despite their handicap. This can be proven by chromosomal structure.

Often, the parents are embarrassed and immediately choose the sex of the child. If they are wrong, then that child will live a life of confusion, always feeling out of place. I do not believe all hermaphrodites are eunuchs, but many choose a gay lifestyle because society does not know how to relate to their differences. Hermaphrodites suffer from physical handicaps that will forever affect them emotionally and spiritually if people are not sensitive to their needs.

Billy has chosen to live as a eunuch because of his physical problem. God gave him instructions in hell that he must go forth and tell His people the truth. Billy told God he couldn't, because he was a man in a woman's body. Billy told the Lord how ashamed he was, and God said, "Go, and tell them. If they have a problem with you, they have a problem with Me!" He assured Billy that his outer appearance was not the issue anymore. God changed Billy's heart and totally delivered him. Billy's testimony is that it is never too late with God!

> I DO NOT BELIEVE ALL HERMAPHRODITES ARE EUNUCHS, BUT MANY CHOOSE A GAY LIFESTYLE BECAUSE SOCIETY DOES NOT KNOW HOW TO RELATE TO THEIR DIFFERENCES.

Billy was also a high-level warlock. He learned the art of witchcraft fluently. He operated in astral projection, water gazing, and palm reading. He is now a faithful member of Spoken Word, and we love him very much. God has taken him from the guttermost to the uttermost. His deliverance is miraculous, and his testimony has stormed the gates of hell.

ADDRESSING THE ISSUE

The spirit of homosexuality is rampant in the church, and it leaves many people in bondage. I have a friend whom the Lord led to minister at a church that we had suspected of supporting same-sex marriage. I went to this church to support my friend in prayer. Long after our trip, we found out that this church was a gay-affirming church. This means they believe that God is a God of love and that He will not send a person to hell over sexual preference.

Apparently, this group deliberately skipped over parts of the Bible. God wiped out the twin cities of Sodom and Gomorrah and surrounding areas, because they were cities of gross sin. These cities were mainly destroyed for their lust for sodomy. Sodomy is anal or oral copulation with someone of the same or opposite sex.

Sodom's residents perverted the rules of sexual intercourse as God had intended. Sexual perversion can also be a reason God wiped out the world with the flood. The Bible says the sons of God came down and had intercourse with the daughters of man. You can read about this in Genesis 6.

Through these sexually perverted acts, giants were born in the earth. The Bible says that when the sons of God came into the daughters of men, they bore children that became mighty men. The word mighty in the Hebrew is *gibbowr*, which means champion giants.

The enemy was attempting to contaminate the human race. The devil tried to destroy the holy seed of the woman. If he had been successful, Jesus wouldn't have come to earth to die for the human race.

Sexual perversion is no secret to God. The Bible says every imagination of the thoughts of man were evil. God repented of making all of creation and said He would destroy man from the face of the earth.

Gay-affirming churches also claim to have a ministry of inclusion. This doctrine says that anyone can receive salvation regardless of race, gender, class, or sexual orientation. The problem with this theory—surely it is not theological—is that God did not include Sodom and Gomorrah or the people before the flood in His plan of salvation.

If the gay affirmers are right, then God will have to repent to Sodom, Gomorrah, and to the people who lived before the flood. Matthew 24:38 teaches that in the days before the flood, people were eating, drinking, marrying, and being given in marriage. The Bible declares that the things the people did before the flood were all evil.

> GOD CHANGED BILLY'S HEART AND TOTALLY DELIVERED HIM. BILLY'S TESTIMONY IS THAT IT IS NEVER TOO LATE WITH GOD!

But what was so evil about marriage? The Lord revealed to me that the key is in the meaning of the word *marrying*. This word in the Greek is *gameo*, and it means to wed of either sex. *Gameo* refers to same-sex marriages! One main reason for the flood is same-sex marriage. God did not put up with it then, and surely those who participate in it today will pay a terrible price.

THE GAY-AFFIRMING CHURCH

The gay-affirming church I went to in support of my friend had a huge campus with thousands of members. I could not tell it was a church that supported homosexuality just from outer appearances. Of course, there were many gay people in attendance, but so are there in many other churches.

I was very proud of my friend as he ministered the unadulterated truth in the devil's camp! Hundreds came to the Lord! He called a little boy to the altar and told him that no matter what anyone told him, he needed role models who would teach him how to be a man. He also told him that when he grew up, he was to marry a wife and that nothing else was acceptable.

Boy, did he give the devil a black eye! The pastor of the church was furious. He told my friend that he did not agree with his interpretation of what traditional churches believe concerning the homosexual lifestyle. He referred to same-sex, loving couples who are claiming salvation.

I say such a thing does not exist. It is like putting winter and summer together. They cannot be combined! It is hot in the summer and cold in the winter. Manifestations of the weather declare the difference.

The perverse lifestyles of homosexuals declare the difference between them and true born-again believers. The pastor of the church rebuked my friend, but I celebrate him. He will get a jewel in his crown in heaven for ministering openly to that little boy.

To add to the story, a friend from my past that I used to get high with in the crack house called me months after I visited this church. His name is Gene. Gene told me the shocking news that the pastor of the gay-affirming church tried to pick him up for a date on the streets.

I asked Gene if there was any way he had mistaken the pastor for a different person. Gene was certain. Though Gene still struggles with crack, he recognized the pastor that day. The preacher had on an Afro wig and was dressed in clothes from the 1960s era. No wonder the church is gay affirming!

I later found out the same pastor was removed from one of the largest churches in our nation for homosexual activity. The greatest sin of America can be found in Romans 1:32:

> Though they are fully aware of God's righteous decree that those who do such things deserve to die, they not only do them themselves but approve and applaud others who practice them.
>
> —AMP

I rest my case!

WITCHCRAFT AND HOMOSEXUALITY

I minister to homosexuals from around the world. There are certain things that tend to go together. It's like beer and football in the world; they go together! Homosexuality and witchcraft walk hand in hand. Gays have told me that they tap into occult arts for things such as love potions.

Time after time, I hear stories about homosexuals. For example, there is one about a preacher who was caught in the very act! He and another man were having sex, and they became physically stuck together like two dogs on the street in heat.

Unfortunately, getting them apart was not as easy as it is for dogs. The two men had to be covered with a sheet and taken to the hospital on a gurney. I know this sounds bizarre, but one of my relatives was in the emergency room the night they arrived.

One of my connections from the dark side told me that the preacher's lover had a wife who suspected him of an affair. She went to a high-level shaman, and he prayed over the liver of a dog and gave it to her to feed to her husband. She cooked it and fed it to him. According to the curse, the next person her husband had sex with, his penis would swell inside the person. She never suspected that it would be a man. Despite this horrible act, the church continued to grow and is a megachurch today.

The church must rise to the occasion and come up against the homosexual agenda in America, but judgment will first start with the house of God!

CHAPTER 4

MOVING ON UP!

ONE DAY I noticed my mom and my aunt Maude bringing new furniture into the house. They said it was for "the new house." What new house? This was dramatic news to us. Where would we move to, and who would be our friends?

I could not imagine not being around the corner from the bar. How would I see the sissy shows? All kinds of fears came to my mind. As my mother tried to comfort us about moving to a better life, we still did not care. What could be better than watching drunks from our apartment window waddle down Beaver Street after the bars had closed?

Uptown's hot asphalt had become our playground. All the movie theaters open to blacks were all located in uptown. The Ritz Theater, the Roosevelt Theater, the Strand Theater, and the Florida Theater were special places for blacks living in Jacksonville, Florida.

Most of the buildings were rat infested, but we had the time of our lives there. My mother told us we were moving to the woods.

This sounded like a horrible place. Who wanted to leave the exciting streets of uptown and move to the woods? Not me!

We moved into a new home in Sherwood Forest on the north side of town. To my surprise, all of my neighbors were white. It was culture shock! I had never interacted with white people in my life. My next-door neighbor was a bus driver. I will never forget her daughter, Helena. Her hair was long and black. I always wanted to touch it, because I had never touched a white girl's hair.

We even attended an integrated school, where white students sat next to me in class. I was very smart in school, and I sat next to a set of white twins named Barbara and Beverly. They were smart also, but something in me told me that I had to be better than the twins. They lived a few blocks from me, and their mom was the only white person who would allow me to play in her home.

All I ever knew about white people was that they treated blacks badly and that their actions and attitudes toward me were proof of that. But my grandmother and grandfather weren't any different. They called white people ugly names. Sadly, when they would talk about whites, you could hear the hatred in their voices. It was always instilled in us to never trust the white man, because he was perceived as a black person's worst enemy.

My aunt Lillie Mae cleaned houses for white people, but I noticed that these people were always nice to her. They never wanted her to leave their home, and they treated her as if she were a part of their family.

Aunt Lillie Mae raised their children as if they were her own children. When she died, they cried harder than I did. This was a seed in my heart that maybe all white people were not bad. But my natural instincts told me to believe what my family instilled in me, not what I saw in the white family my aunt worked for.

Eventually, we got used to our new neighbors, but they never got used to us. Within a few years, the white people in our neighborhood moved out of Sherwood like a tornado was coming. It seemed like overnight that it became a predominantly black neighborhood. Only very poor whites remained in the neighbor-hood, because they could not afford to leave.

By this time in my life, my sisters and I were being recognized for our athletic abilities. My middle sister, Thabathia, and I were exceptionally intelligent girls. We were placed in advanced courses and made good grades. We excelled. I was also an honor roll student who won every essay contest I entered. I was confident in who I was.

But the junior high school I attended frequently had race riots, and of course, I was on the front lines inciting and initiating trouble. I will never forget when a large group of my friends jumped on a white boy for throwing a brick at our bus. I was the first to beat him up.

I can remember grabbing him by his hair and pulling it from the roots of his scalp. I was in a rage. I cursed and kicked him. Sadly, I had no sense of guilt about my actions. In fact, I found it rather enjoyable like Big Momma did when the rapist broke into our home. What prompted me to stop beating the boy were the lice in his hair. When I grabbed his hair, I looked at it in my hand; it was infested with lice. I stopped fighting and ran off wishing I could have kicked him just one more time.

FAMILIAR SPIRITS

The same year we moved to Sherwood Forest, my grandmother died. My grandfather always seemed to have few words after she died. I was sad for him and the rest of the family, but I didn't cry. I loved Big Momma deep inside, but it was a relief to not have to be her eyes and hands any longer. Still, it seemed as though she was holding on to my shoulder for guidance. Now I know that what felt like her hands were actually the same spirits that had once controlled her. They were now my guide.

Proof of their existence in me was obvious. I was forced to walk close to my grandmother, and later I found myself acting just like her. I cursed fluently and would do so to the point of making another person cry. Fighting was a part of my soul, because it came natural to my mind. If I did not have a fight at least once a week, I felt like something was missing in my life.

I even started a gang with a group of the toughest girls in my school. We did not call ourselves by any particular name, but our actions spoke for us. Everybody in the group had a day to fight somebody. If the person whose day it was to fight could not find an innocent bystander to jump on, we would turn around and fight her.

Even though my family left uptown, uptown never left me! Whenever I had confrontations, I could hear my grandmother's voice in my head: "Never let them hit you first. Always strike first, and ask questions later!" I lived by that law. Blacks from the uptown area moved to Sherwood Forest and other surrounding neighborhoods. The cycle started all over again, and our neighborhood became a suburban uptown.

BLAZING A TRAIL

The junior high school I attended never had a black student to win student council president or homecoming queen. That annoyed me. I did not like it that blacks were never voted for these positions, and I decided to do something about it. I entered my name on the ballot.

I always knew I was born to make a difference in the world. It was not important to me at the time about what I was born to do; I just knew it was "something." I was sure that if what I was doing did not fit the mold, I could break the old mold and create a new one. I knew even as a child I was a catalyst for change.

I have never had a problem challenging the status quo. It's something God had to place in me. I really believe this is why God recruited me for His kingdom. He knew that if I believed in something strong enough, I would not stop until the job was done! And if I didn't meet people's expectations of me, oh well!

I figured out a strategy to win homecoming queen by taking advantage of being one of two black girls on the ballot. I thought, *All the pretty white girls will have to split their votes.* My strategy worked. Only one other black girl entered the contest, and she was not popular enough to make a difference.

I became the first black homecoming queen at Highlands Junior High School in Jacksonville, Florida. The momentum from my win had a domino effect in my life. I was also voted president of a 95 percent white student council.

Neither of those titles meant anything to me. I got my thrill from winning. I couldn't care less about school politics, and all I wanted was my picture in the yearbook as homecoming queen. In fact, a few months after I had won, I pulled the fire alarm and was stripped of both titles as punishment.

I ALWAYS KNEW I WAS BORN TO MAKE A DIFFERENCE IN THE WORLD. IT WAS NOT IMPORTANT TO ME AT THE TIME ABOUT WHAT I WAS BORN TO DO, I JUST KNEW IT WAS "SOMETHING." I WAS SURE THAT IF WHAT I WAS DOING DID NOT FIT THE MOLD, I COULD BREAK THE OLD MOLD AND CREATE A NEW ONE. I KNEW EVEN AS A CHILD I WAS A CATALYST FOR CHANGE.

I graduated from Highlands and went to Jean Ribault Senior High School, home of the Trojans. My high school experience was similar to my junior high years; I excelled academically and athletically. But despite my success, the dean of girls was constantly on my trail. She was a black, middle-aged woman with a strong personality. She talked a lot of "noise" to students like me. Though I never got caught, her suspicions of me let her know I was a troublemaker. She would walk on the top of the school building—in a dress—holding a megaphone and yelling at me as I escaped through the school's barbed wire fence while skipping classes.

I was so wild that in the twelfth grade, I made straight As the first three quarters, quit school the last quarter, and still managed to graduate with a C average. Despite the dean's disapproval, I entered the races for homecoming queen and president of student council and won both.

During my school years, I had very little supervision in my home. I went to school when I wanted, came home as late as I wanted, and smoked cigarettes in my mother's face. My sisters and I were cooking our own meals, and we literally took care of ourselves. Though my mom worked and paid the bills, we were evicted from our home, causing me much embarrassment as a teenager. By age fourteen, I would leave my house on Friday, and I would return Sunday. By the time my mom figured out I was in trouble, it was too late.

My Teen Years

As I grew into my teen years, I eventually became so rebellious that my mother sought help to get me under control. She wasn't a saved woman, so she knew nothing about the spirit of witchcraft. When I was fourteen, things occurred in my life that have been etched in my memory. For starters, my mother married a man who was seven years older than me. We argued constantly, and I couldn't stand him.

One of my mom's "friends," Wilamena, suggested to my mother that she take me to "someone." This so-called "someone" was a "root man" (a person who practices witchcraft). She took me to a house and left me in the room with that big, black ugly man. To be honest, he looked like a grizzly bear.

Though my mom did what Wilamena told her, she later repented to me for taking me to the root man. She told me that as the man grew older, he was constantly being tormented by demons and that he died a horrible death. Take heed, reader; the end of sin is always death!

The room was very small, and it was furnished with a small table and lamp in the center of the room. The root man's eyes were bloodshot red, and he had very big lips. He began to tell me things about myself that were true. He asked me if I wanted to be the fastest woman in the world. He offered to give me a bottle and said that if I put it in my bath, I would be the fastest woman in the world.

I hesitantly gave it some thought, but I said no. Something told me that I didn't give him the answer he wanted to hear. After I left the root man, my life started going on a downward path. It was as if I had told the devil no, and he vowed to make me pay for it.

Less than a year later of leaving the man's house, I found myself pregnant. I was only in the tenth grade. This was a very confusing time in my life. I had no one to turn to, so I went to the hospital alone to have an abortion. As I was being admitted, the nurse discovered that I was only fifteen.

I will never forget the look on her face when she said, "Baby, you need to call your mother!" I had the abortion, and it was a horrible experience. My horrible experience was compounded with the doctor's negligence. He failed to completely terminate my pregnancy, leaving part of my baby inside me.

When I returned to school a few days after the abortion, I realized my baby's remains were literally coming out of me. It was painful and gross! When the dean who had been running me down with a megaphone found me in the bathroom standing in a pool of blood, even her heart went out to me.

The blood of Jesus covers me today concerning what I did to this baby. My comfort is that my child is in heaven, and God has thrown my sin into the sea of forgetfulness.

CHAPTER 5

INTRODUCTION TO WITCHCRAFT

M Y SISTERS AND I enjoyed our years in Sherwood Forest, but they soon came to an end when my family moved to an area called Forest Hills. My adolescent years were tough, and I really needed my mother's guidance. I would often stay out until 6:00 a.m. on the weekends and midnight on school nights. Sometimes my mother would open the door, and I would fall into the house deliriously drunk. I never particularly liked alcohol. But during this time in my life, I turned to it as a result of peer pressure.

As a single woman, my mother was always working to take care of her three girls, but that didn't stop her from living her own life. She had divorced the young man she married, and, once again, our household consisted of just women.

She had friends who would come to visit regularly. One night around 11:00 p.m., her friend questioned her about me leaving the house at such a late hour. I boldly interrupted the conversation to let them know that where I was going was none of their business! My mother politely asked them to leave me alone.

I often heard my mother's new friends tell her that there was something "special" about me. As it turned out, these new associates were nothing more than modern-day witches. In fact, nice people under the control of witchcraft often infiltrate the body of Christ.

My exposure as a young girl to my mother's friends from the dark side planted a seed in me. I began to hate witchcraft with a passion. In my present ministry, God has given me a burden and an assignment to confront witches with His truth. It is only the truth that will make them free.

WILAMENA AND THE MAGICAL NUMBERS

One of my mom's friends, Wilamena, and I were always in conflict with each other. She never set right with me, and I knew the feeling was mutual. She was the one who would always call me "special." She lived in a big house a few blocks from ours. Even in the daytime, she burned candles all over her house.

Wilamena's house was always filthy, and my mom sent us over to help her clean it. It was so junky that the more we cleaned it, the worse it looked. After we cleaned for hours, instead of paying us money, she fed us. If I had known then what I know now, I would have never eaten from that table. The food looked strange, and the portions were very small. I told my sisters we needed to leave that house and never return.

Something about that woman made me hate to even hear her name—*Wilamena*. I later discovered that she used occult powers to give people numbers for gambling. She also had followers who considered her their spiritual "bishop." She had churches in several cities, yet she didn't attend church herself. She cursed like a sailor and smoked cigarettes. What kind of bishop was this?

Once, I watched as Wilamena tied rags around a broom that had a flammable liquid on it. She lit a match to it and rolled it up and down my mother's back. The skin did not burn, but it turned a sooty black. As real as it seemed, I do not remember if this was a dream or vision, or if I really saw it. My mother did say that Wilamena and other women tried to cast demons out of her.

They placed my mother in the bathtub and poured ammonia on her. No demons came out of her, but my mother was badly burned as a result of the incident.

UNMASKING THE DEVIL'S TACTICS

During one Christmas season, I can remember when my mom and the women struck it rich at the dog races. They took $100 bills and placed the money in what appeared to be water. They thought that putting the money in water would make it multiply. But instead of multiplying as intended, the money actually decreased—because I stole $300 and went shopping! I quickly caught the bus to the mall, and I smiled as I proudly wore my new coat and boots. Everybody else involved was broke again.

Oddly, I hated the dog races with a passion, because the dogs at the racetrack lived and ate better than I did. We lost two homes to gambling, and fortunately that is a demon I have never entertained as an adult.

A FATHER TO THE FATHERLESS

As an older woman, my mother married another man, Joseph Doddie. We affectionately called him Doddie. Back in the 1980s I knew nothing about being part of a blended family, and it showed. My sisters and I often had horrible rumbles with Doddie and his grown children. His children would call my mom a gold digger, because she was much younger than he was.

It came to me that if my mom was digging for gold when she said "I do," she could have dug for someone with a little more money. Doddie wasn't filthy rich. He was a middle-class, hardworking man. Still, his money was never enough to pay for my mother's gambling habit.

Eventually, Doddie became the only man we considered a father.

He was the only grandfather my children ever knew. But despite his willingness to be there for us, he was not the easiest man to get along with. Though we would cuss him out and wouldn't speak to him for weeks at a time, we would always iron out our differences and continue to love on him.

When I gave my life to Jesus, Doddie watched me for years to see if my conversion was authentic. He would always joke with me about the people who attended his church. He was convinced that the only people who went to the same church were sissies and politicians. And he was the most carnally minded man I knew. He would get fresh with all of my female preacher friends who came by the house.

But today, I am proud to say that as Doddie watched me to see if I was really saved, God miraculously saved him! He became a highly respected person in the city. Before he died, he would lay back in his easy chair and worship God with tears streaming down his face. On his deathbed, Doddie's last request was that all of his children reconcile with each other and serve God.

Before dying, he also told me how he renounced the witchcraft he was involved in with Rev. Smith, a man who pretended to be a preacher. My mom once told me Doddie took her to see a root man, because Rev. Smith told him to. She said it was the most horrible experience in her life.

The root man, who had dark skin and fire red eyes, worked his voodoo in a spooky hut, according to my mom. Doddie had initially taken my mom to the man in hopes that he could stop her itching. When Doddie died, I was on the road preaching at a major conference. But I later called Rev. Smith and told him I knew he was a warlock and that he would pay if he spoke one word over my daddy's body.

I explained to him that Doddie had repented and renounced him and his witchcraft before he died. Rev. Smith came to the funeral, but when the ministers were given an opportunity to speak about my father, the reverend dared not say a word.

WALKING IN THE SPIRIT

God will not allow us to be ignorant of the devices of the enemy. He gives us a strong defense. Any army without good secret intelligence agents will not be successful! I am so glad God has given us the Holy Spirit, who gives us information concerning the dark side of the spiritual realm. He does this so His people can sense the wiles of the devil.

Despite what I know about the dark side, it is still hard for me to believe people willingly serve the devil. My mother wanted the benefits of hanging out with witchcraft practitioners, but she never truly wanted to give her soul to Satan.

Like so many other people, she didn't realize that it was a package deal. When she recognized who she was really dealing with, she walked out on her longtime buddies. God had to open her eyes to what she was engaged in.

Once, my mother unexpectedly went to Wilamena's house on her lunch break. The door was cracked, so my mom walked in unannounced. When she peeped in, she found Wilamena bowing before an altar naked and rubbing something on the floor. Cloaked in a black cloth, the altar had a statue of Mary and baby Jesus. When my mother asked Wilamena what was she doing, Wilamena said, "Getting niggers off of my back!"

Wilamena's response was in a deep voice that

> PEOPLE WHO WHISPER SPELLS TO ENCHANT OR CONTROL OTHERS SHOULD NOT BE ORDAINED OR PERMITTED TO OPERATE.

was not her own. The demons that spoke through this woman told my mother they needed her to join them to complete the ritual. Wilamena promised my mom that the "group" she was with would give her power like Jim Jones. Wilamena adored Jim Jones and often spoke of how wonderful he was. I have not seen Wilamena since I met Jesus, but I trust that the day will come when I can look her directly in her eyes and tell her Jesus is Lord—join Him or die! Exodus 22:18 says that a witch should not be suffered to live.

> WHEN PEOPLE HAVE AFFLICTIONS THAT ARE ROOTED IN WITCHCRAFT, MEDICAL SCIENCE CANNOT DETERMINE THE SOURCE. YOU CAN'T SOLVE A SPIRITUAL PROBLEM WITH NATURAL MEANS. AS I OFTEN TELL PEOPLE, "IF YOU'VE GOT A DEVIL PROBLEM, YOU NEED A JESUS ANSWER!"

The Hebrew translation of the word *suffer* is *nathan,* which means to lift up, recompense, grant, ordain, render, or send out. The translation for *witch* is *kashaph,* and it means to whisper a spell, to enchant or control the minds of people, or to operate in any power that is not Holy Spirit–initiated and controlled. In other words, people who whisper spells to enchant or control others should not be ordained or permitted to operate. I agree with the Word: "I suffer a witch not to live!"

The ladies my mother used to associate with still operate in witchcraft, yet deep down inside they know Jesus is greater. They are gamblers who not only take a chance with their money, but they also take chances with their souls!

One of the women, Ms. Ruby, actually came to know Jesus. She was a small black woman who operated fluently in witchcraft. One day, she announced to the others in the witchcraft group that she had chosen Jesus and asked them to forgive her if she had trespassed against them in any way.

One lady named Tessa refused to forgive her and hated her immensely for accepting the Lord. My mother heard the woman say that before the sun went down, Ms. Ruby would pay. Ms. Ruby started dying so quickly that the doctors could not keep up with all her ailments.

Her organs began to fail. I was not saved at the time, and Ms. Ruby did not know anyone who was knowledgeable or powerful enough to help her escape the demonic calling she had received as a witch. Even though she died a torturous death, I believe she sincerely came to Christ before she died and is now resting in the presence of the Lord. Tessa recently died a tormenting death.

When people have afflictions that are rooted in witchcraft, medical science cannot determine the source. You can't solve a spiritual problem with natural means. As I often tell people, "If you've got a devil problem, you need a Jesus answer!"

I praise God that He has given us power over the devil. You can't be "rooted" by the root man if you are rooted and grounded in Christ. You should not be afraid of witchcraft, but never deny its existence.

God does not want us to be ignorant of the enemy's devices. God said in His Word that His people perish for a lack of knowledge. Many prominent preachers have died early deaths in my city, this is why we must watch as well as pray!

CHAPTER 6

I'm Coming Out!

BEFORE I GRADUATED from high school, I met a young man who asked me to live with him and to have his baby. He was twenty-three and had many girlfriends, but I needed a change in environment, so I accepted his offer.

My mother almost passed out when I went to her job and told her I was planning to have Michael's baby. We literally went to her job and asked for her permission. I know it was a terrible thing to do, because I was only seventeen. But I really cared for him, and I knew he would be a good provider. He had proved that to me by paying all of my high school expenses, including graduation. I really loved him, but I had not taken the time to learn to love myself.

Today I appreciate how Michael provided for my baby and me. The problem was, he became the father that I never had, and who needs to marry their father?

Needless to say, I graduated from high school pregnant. Again, I had to resign from my positions of homecoming queen and student council. I still had the consolation of winning, though,

65

and my pictures were already in the yearbook.

During my senior year at Ribault, I missed out on prom, grad night, and other special activities a normal teen would have given anything to do. I had to force myself to walk down the aisle to receive my diploma—six months pregnant. Even though I was expecting, I still purchased a yearbook, because the memories of my successes in high school meant a lot to me.

DELIVERANCE FROM THE FAMILIAR

I lived such a fast life in high school that I never reached my athletic potential. Accepting the offer to have my boyfriend's baby, I lost the opportunity to obtain a track scholarship. Though my baby's father, Michael, was very successful in his career and was an excellent provider, something was still missing. Hesitantly, I followed him to Portland, Oregon, on a job transfer. All I had was my son, my clothes, and an approved financial aid packet for college.

Oregon was the cleanest place I had every seen. As a matter of fact, it was too clean. There was no ghetto, no uptown, and no sissies. I did not think I would make it in Oregon. I had a perfect little family, except I was a common law wife, which meant I wasn't married!

All I had to do was say the word, and my boyfriend would have been happy to have everything legalized, but something in me said no. I had escaped my mother's house only to come under the supervision of my boyfriend. He had the responsibility of picking up where my mother left off, but no one knew where she left off. There was a missing link! My body had committed to a relationship that my mind was not willing to live up to.

Michael handled everything. My life consisted of taking care of the house and putting things on layaway at the mall for him to get out. Everything was so nice and in place that it began to make me sick. I literally missed the dirt from uptown. I would have paid anything to hang out uptown just one more time. I missed "shootin' the breeze" with my homosexual friends. If there were any gay people in the city, they were definitely in the closet! In Oregon, even what they called the ghetto was nice!

I convinced Michael that if something did not change, I was going back to Florida. Since I could not enjoy the street life I was addicted to, there was only one other joy that could fill my soul—track and field! I loved to run, and I knew I could do it very well. Michael took me to the community college in Mount Hood, Oregon. I had never seen mountains before. All I could think about was how my street friends would trip out on the scenery.

As soon as I arrived on the campus of Mt. Hood Community College, I headed straight for the track office. I walked in and introduced myself to the head coach. I had no idea this man had connections with the Olympic Advisory Board. After introducing myself, I told the coach I was enrolling in his school and would run for his team under certain conditions.

I told him I would pay for my schooling one quarter, but I wanted a full scholarship for the winter term. I promised him I would outrun every woman on his team. He told me that if I outran every woman on his team, he would give me anything I wanted. My new coach was Jim Puckett, and to this day, he tells the story of how the key to a national championship walked into his office.

Just a few weeks had passed, and I broke every school sprint record for women. I was running with a speed I had never known before, and soon I qualified for the nationals. I was finally running at my maximum potential. For the moment, uptown was no longer on my mind. I grabbed a hold of the vision that I was a national champion, for real!

Everything was happening so fast. Jim Puckett was an influential man, and he pulled strings to get me in a popular televised meet. My event was the 60-meter indoors, and it was like the grand finale for the night.

My baby's father had never seen me run. He managed a concession company in the coliseum and stood in the corridor on his break to watch the race. They turned the lights out and put a spotlight on every competitor. One by one, the announcer read each person's accomplishments and titles in track and field. When it came to me, the commentator merely said, "In this lane, we have Kim Parrish." I was nobody on the track and field circuit, but I had a determination in my heart to be a winner.

The gun went off. In a matter of seconds, I blew everybody on the entire field off the track. Everybody was wondering where I had come from. I believe this was the night when my baby's father realized I would not be with him forever.

LIFE IN THE FAST LANE

Every time I stepped on the track, my legs moved faster, my head got bigger, and my temper ran hotter. I was one of two blacks on the team, and there were only a handful of blacks in the entire college. The assistant track coach was black and a real "brother." He made me feel comfortable on the team, even though my dialect clearly separated me from him and my teammates.

Even the other blacks in the college were a lot different from me. They acted more "white" in their speech and mannerisms, and they would often giggle at the way I talked. My ghetto-country accent also made it very embarrassing for me to ask questions in class. Despite my challenges, I refused to change just to be like everybody else. I could have tried to talk like everyone else, but I took pride in being me.

At the end of the first semester, I had a 3.65 grade point average, a heavy academic load, a baby, housework, a part-time job, track practice, travel, and a live-in man to tend to. I was determined to be all I could be, but I depended solely on "self" to accomplish my goals. My coach would take me to local Kiwanis meetings to introduce me to people who donated money to the college. These meetings were held at 6:00 a.m., once a week.

I tried to ignore my coach's knock at my apartment door at 5:00

a.m. Most of the time, I wasn't dressed when he arrived. I was hiding, because I did not want to attend what I called his "Ku Klux Klan" meetings. I wondered if the name Kiwanis was a front for the organization. I was afraid those white people would take a detour down a dark road before daybreak and lynch me. I also wondered if one of his lodge members would have a flashback and have an old-fashioned lynching!

But my thoughts about white people were very different from my boyfriend's. Michael worked for a company that had all white employees—with the exception of him—but it didn't bother him, because he was very comfortable with them. Michael was an intelligent, well-spoken guy, so the way I presented myself in public sometimes embarrassed him.

There were times when the police would drag me past Michael's office in the coliseum, because the spirit of my grandmother would overcome me and I would start fighting. One of the employees asked Michael, "Hey, man, wasn't that your wife the police just dragged past the door?" Though my boyfriend often kept me out of trouble, he was the person who would drag me out of bed to go to those Kiwanis meetings. I felt like I was the "token nigger" on the track team.

SURVIVING CULTURE SHOCK

It wasn't just the college's lack of diversity that made me hate it; everything about Oregon was culture shock for me. Not having my family and not being able to attend the "sissy shows" left me very homesick.

Oregon had one radio station called KABU that aired black music one hour on Sunday. That was the highlight of my week. I had a problem with white people, and I most definitely had a problem with their music, but eventually I became a hard-core rock music fan.

Once, when I was traveling with the team, we stopped at an

Indian reservation in the mountains. Because of the intense hatred for blacks in that area, everyone advised me not to get off the bus. Even though I was raised "uptown," I was not a fool. I stayed low on the bus and asked them to please hurry back with my food. What kind of place was this that a track star could not eat in a restaurant with the rest of the team?

While I was waiting on the bus I saw an old lady's grocery basket rolling down a hill and getting away from her. I ran from the bus to save her basket from crashing. As I caught the grocery basket, she yelled, "Nigger, do not touch my basket." I could not believe the hatred I saw in her wrinkled eyes. I will never forget that day. I realized that racism was deeper than I could imagine. It was one thing to be in race riots, but the feeling I felt that day in the grocery store parking lot, all alone and so far from home, was indescribable.

As I continued to run track, I eventually qualified to run four events in junior college nationals. One day after practice, a female runner named Dawn sat in the whirlpool with me. She was a full-blooded Cherokee Indian and a pretty good athlete. When I pulled my leg out of the ice, it was purple. She yelled, "Look at your leg; you're really a nigger there!" It took everything in me not to drown her in that whirlpool. I rehearsed it so many times in my head that, to this day, I cannot remember if I pushed her head under the water or not.

I made a vow to break her legs after the national meet, and I meant it. When I first got on the team, Dawn and the white athletes thought it was perfectly normal to call me a nigger. After getting to know me better I would hear them say to each other, "Whatever you do, don't call Kim a nigger—she doesn't like that!"

I tried to correct my teammates through threats and physical abuse. Many times I found myself cursing like my grandmother did, and those in my college swore they had never heard such vulgar things. Several times I cornered teammates in the shower room, promising to beat them down after nationals. From the coaches on down, I was increasingly regarded as a crazy person.

Hollow Victories

Junior College Nationals were held in San Angelo, Texas, where it was 105 degrees in the shade. Most of my teammates could not handle the humidity, but I was right at home. As our bus transported us from the airport and we approached the campus where the meet was held, my eyes lit up with excitement. Black people were everywhere! I felt like kissing the ground.

One of my teammates yelled, "Gollee, would ya look at the niggers!" By this time I was tired of fighting and understood their ignorance. I remember promising myself, "I'm going to be the fastest nigger in the nation!"

Some of you may not understand how I can freely use the word *nigger* like I do; it's because the Son makes you free, and I am free indeed!

God killed that word in my heart while I was living in Oregon. It got to the point where white people could no longer control my behavior by calling me that name. I was not a nigger, and I refused to respond to that name anymore. Some people do not get the revelation of how God will take the devil's evil intentions for your life and work it for your good. Today, I see white boys give black boys high fives and say, "Whuz up, my nigga!" Ain't nobody mad about it but the devil!

Walking in the Limelight

At nationals it seemed that every time I hit the track, I broke a record. The newspapers interviewed a young lady from Nebraska and asked her what she thought about me and the way I was running. She confidently stated that I would burn out by finals and that she would win the gold. Nobody interviewed me, but I knew those gold medals had my name on them.

I won first place in three races, beating the Nebraska sprinter and anyone else who stepped on the track. It was my season. It seemed like I could not lose. At the end of the day, my coach announced that I was anchoring the 4 x 400 relay, but I really didn't want to. I was already in shock from winning the 4 x 100 relay with three white girls running the first three legs. This was unheard of!

Everybody knows white girls can't sprint. They were the only white girls on the track, and everybody else was black. But to my surprise, they passed me the baton in first place. Three white girls and one black won the National Junior College 4 x 100 relay, and I could not take all the glory. I already had it made up in my mind that I would get the baton last and run everybody down. It is not until now that I realized how vain I was. Those white girls showed me something that day, and I learned a great lesson. We are living in a day where white girls can run and white boys can jump! God gives gifts to whom He pleases.

Yet my coach was trying to take the same four people and win the 4 x 400.

> GOD KILLED THAT WORD IN MY HEART WHILE I WAS LIVING IN OREGON. IT GOT TO THE POINT WHERE WHITE PEOPLE COULD NO LONGER CONTROL MY BEHAVIOR BY CALLING ME THAT NAME. SOME PEOPLE DO NOT GET THE REVELATION OF HOW GOD WILL TAKE THE DEVIL'S EVIL INTENTIONS FOR YOUR LIFE AND WORK IT FOR YOUR GOOD. TODAY, I SEE WHITE BOYS GIVE BLACK BOYS HIGH FIVES AND SAY, "WHUZ UP, MY NIGGA!" AIN'T NOBODY MAD ABOUT IT BUT THE DEVIL!

Lightning cannot strike twice in the same place! But it did. I was given the award for the Most Outstanding Female Athlete in the nation. After calling home to let everyone know what had taken place, I forgave the white girls who had called me nigger during the season. That meant I had nothing to look forward to, not even a good fight.

I went back to my room and cried after all that great victory, because I still felt a void in my life. *There must be more to life than this!* I kept saying to myself. I know for a fact that the superstars you see in the sports and entertainment industry are not as happy as you might think. Life without Jesus is miserable to everybody!

NATIONAL CHAMPIONSHIPS

My coach talked me into running in the U.S. National Championships. The good part was that I got to go home to Florida to train for a month before competition. At least I thought it was good. The Bible says there is a way that seems right to a man, but the end of it is death.

That summer I packed my bags, grabbed my baby, and went back to Florida. I took as much as I could carry on the plane. My baby's father, Michael, thought I was only going home for training. I did not have the nerve to tell him that I had no intention of returning to Oregon. All I could see ahead of me were open doors, but I had no idea I was headed for a dead end.

Training did not go well in Florida. Trying to live a double life again distracted me. I tried to fit the club, uptown, and the sissy shows into my training schedule. I even got to experience the desire of my heart—to live with my natural father. He had another girlfriend, named Ruth, and she had a daughter from him named Connie. For the first time in my life, I felt like Perk's daughter. A newspaper article came out about my track accomplishments, and it recognized me as Perk's daughter. This was my dream come true to live with my real father.

Perk drove me to Orlando, and I flew out to Sacramento, California, for the American Team Nationals. During the month I was home for training, I had received scholarship offers from almost every state in the nation. I could have gone anywhere, but I wanted to be a part of the best sprint team in the nation, which at the time was Florida State University. But when I pursued Florida State, it was the only college that did not show interest in me.

Big names and bright lights brought distraction to the effectiveness of my race at the nationals. I ran poor times, worse than I had run all season.

A New Man

Chandra Cheeseborough was a three-time Olympian and my teammate in high school. She introduced me to all the big-name runners, but there was one I would never forget. Marcus Riley was a world-class, 200-meter champion and fit well into my goal of snatching a famous athlete. I had already cut ties with my baby's father, and I immediately flipped over Marcus. He appeared to have the same feelings for me.

One day I had a brief encounter at the airport with the head track coach for Florida State University. Fortunately for me, everything turned around that day. With a position on FSU's track team, I went back home and spent the summer with my sissies and kept in contact with Marcus, long distance, at my dad's expense.

In the fall semester I packed my bags and moved to Tallahassee. For the first time, I was separated from my son. I was also on my own. There was no daddy, momma, or boyfriend to watch over me. Michael begged me to leave our son, Mike-Mike, with his parents. I knew this was best for my child, and something in me wanted to be free.

Meanwhile, I moved in with Marcus. He was a very neat man. He was a model and bragged on himself all the time. He only wore designer clothing, and what people thought of him meant more than anything to him. We had an awesome relationship, because we were best friends.

Once again, though, I simply did not fit the mold. Marcus and I spent a lot of time together at the beginning of our relationship, but it eventually declined. Girls that had previous relationships with him would frequently come to the door crying, and he would treat them so badly. I felt sorry for them, but there was nothing I could do to help them ... he was *my* man!

Marcus was very jealous and never wanted me around other men. We began to have violent encounters, and I was exposed to all the other women he had besides me. Marcus and I broke up, and I moved into my own apartment. It was not long before I found myself crying on the other side of Marcus's door, with someone else on the inside with him.

My obsession with Marcus was really a distraction to my track career. All my dreams were going down the drain. My coaches soon began to lose confidence in me, and I knew that it would not be long before I would lose my scholarship.

I was on the fastest relay team in the nation, but my nightlife was faster than my track life; the other girls left me behind on the field. They were disciplined and focused, and track was their god. I was soon replaced and became an alternate on the team. I ran against the young lady whom I had beat at Junior College Nationals. She was on the University of Nebraska track team. She blew me off the track, and I sat in the stands crying in front of everyone there.

I was at an all time low while three girls from the relay team that I was once on went to the Olympics. I was, unfortunately, left behind.

CHAPTER 7

FROM CRAZY
TO THE CRACK HOUSE

M Y RELATIONSHIP WITH Marcus was like a yo-yo. His violent outbursts were so bad the coaches barred him from the track field. I can remember the day he beat me for having a football player in my apartment.

He loved having other women in his life, but he could not stand the idea of me being with another man. In retaliation, I caught Marcus from behind and beat him like Big Momma used to beat my granddaddy. Still, Marcus got the best of me and beat me until I was almost unconscious. But as he proudly walked away with his back to me, the spirit of my grandmother rose up within me to give him a good beat-down!

After I attacked him from behind, I got a knife from the kitchen drawer and cut the convertible top to his brand-new car into pieces. I was very discreet about my abusive situation. If I had made a few phone calls to uptown, Marcus's woman-beating program would have ceased immediately.

Eventually, Marcus's drama affected my performance. I lost my scholarship, and I left the track team with two years of NCAA eligibility left. I vowed that one day I would return. As it turned out, I never competed again, but God did something more awesome than I could have ever imagined.

Today, as I share my story, my son Mike-Mike is the second fastest quarter-mile runner ever at Florida State University besides Olympian Walter McCoy. What the devil stole from me, I received back through my seed. And being just a regular student at FSU was an easy life to adapt to. I missed track and field, but as long as I stayed away from it, I was fine. I never watched it on television, because it caused a deep emptiness inside me.

The Crazy House

One day, my roommate and I played a trick on Marcus to make him think I was trying to commit suicide. Something in me vied for his attention, and I thought this would be the ultimate attention getter. I emptied a bottle of pills and hid them under the bathroom counter. I told my roommate what I had done, but when Marcus arrived at my apartment, she seemed to have forgotten what I told her.

When Marcus found me, he stuck his fingernails in my side until I was bleeding and walked me to his car. He insisted on taking me to the hospital. Even though I begged him to believe I had not swallowed those pills, he was determined not to listen.

Marcus called my coach, and they convinced me to sign papers to be treated for attempted suicide. I later learned they had actually invoked the Baker Act and had me admitted to a mental ward.

The hospital gave me medicine designed to pump my stomach, but all I could do was violently throw up dry heave, because nothing was there. Marcus got in his car to go home to another woman as I was checked into a mental hospital.

The doctor explained to me that anytime there was a threat of suicide, they had to keep the patient overnight. It finally hit me that I was being committed to a crazy house. I could not believe it!

The intake counselor looked like a mad scientist from a creature-feature movie, but his appearance didn't stop me from trying to get released. I tried to convince him that the entire situation was a mistake, but he assured me I wouldn't be released without his permission.

The weirdness of uptown was nothing compared to this place. I knew I had to sleep at night, so I tried not to stir up anything or make enemies. I had good reason to be on my best behavior. There were murderers, anorexics, and reprobates in this strange hospital, and I knew that I didn't fit in.

As I stood at the doors of the elevator crying, I noticed a woman standing in a padded room holding a straitjacket. In an eerie voice she said, "Little girl, why are you here? Little girl, come to me. Little girl!" When I didn't respond, her voice changed to a deep male voice, and she began to curse me with words I had never heard uptown. As I look back, I now understand that she was full of demons.

BACK TO THE STREETS

After leaving the mental hospital, I moved from my nice apartment to a drug-infested neighborhood in the city near a place called French Town. Finally, I was at home again. French Town was just like uptown, but college students did not hang out there. Soon, word got out around the college that I had become a street person. But my friends failed to realize that this *was* the real me, not something I had become. What had been deeply embedded in me was drawing me in.

As usual, it wasn't long before I started dating again. He was a bus driver and very cute, but he wasn't street savvy like me. Through my relationship with the bus driver, I met another bus driver named Danny.

Danny was a drug dealer from the streets of Belle Glade, Florida. Back then, I considered Belle Glade the ghetto of ghettos. But I liked Danny, because he was just my speed. He was fast on the streets, talked my language, and was the most handsome man I'd ever met.

Danny and his live-in girlfriend had a baby boy. Even though Danny was already taken, we became partners in crime. We did whatever we could to make money quick, and we had fun doing it.

Danny, unlike Marcus, treated me special. The problem was, he had two or three houses that he kept other women in. But it didn't matter, because I liked the way he treated me when we were together. Deep down inside the fear of him leaving me was there, yet I refused to entertain it.

INTRODUCTION TO FREEBASE

During this time, the drug *crack* was not introduced. What you know today as crack was called "base cocaine," which was also known as "freebase." The people who abused it were known as "freebasers." So from this point on, whenever I refer to "crack," I am actually talking about freebase.

As I went on with my life, I met a drug dealer named Carlos who worked at FSU. He had been trying to get me to his house for months, but I wouldn't go, because I knew what he really wanted. Carlos was known for getting women high on dope and then taking advantage of them. My roommate became one of his victims, and she hung out with him often.

One day, he begged my roommate to lure me to his house. Though I was streetwise, I was more innocent when it came to the sex scene. I was a drug dealer's dream come true. I knew I had to be very cautious, because the men were notorious for getting women hooked on drugs and having orgies with them.

There was a time when Danny and I were not seeing much of each other. As a result, I started seeing other guys. But they bored me, because all the while I kept seeing Danny's face. When my roommate called me to come to Carlos's house and smoke cocaine,

I had a young man at my apartment. This young man was a pharmacist and drove an awesome Porsche.

At first I wasn't interested in my roommate's offer to join her to smoke cocaine, but I eventually gave in to the peer pressure. The guy with me begged me not to go, insisting that I didn't know what I was about to do to myself. Despite his plea, I made him drop me off at Carlos's house.

As we entered the driveway, the pharmacist shocked me by begging me to let him come along. It turned out that he was an undercover junkie. This is why he could warn me so well. Undercover junkies are the worst kind. They hide behind their professions as doctors, lawyers, pharmacists, and even preachers. They are no different from street junkies; they're just "rock stars" with an occupation.

On the streets we call them "functional junkies." They're strung out, but they somehow manage to keep their nine-to-five jobs. Ardell and I have spent the night smoking dope with surgeons and then watched them go to the hospital to perform surgery on a patient. There are judges who preside over cases, lawyers who represent clients, and dentists who pull teeth while they're all high on dope.

> UNDERCOVER JUNKIES ARE THE WORST KIND. THEY HIDE BEHIND THEIR PROFESSIONS AS DOCTORS, LAWYERS, PHARMACISTS, AND EVEN PREACHERS.

I walked into Carlos's house and found my roommate and another girl half-naked. The entire environment seemed strange to me, and I asked my roommate why she was naked. Then they put a pipe to my mouth and asked me whether I felt anything. I did not feel a thing, and I was getting quite uncomfortable about the entire ordeal.

Although I had not seen Danny for some time, I called him and asked him to come to the house, because I was afraid. Carlos and Danny hit it off fine, because they were in the same game—drugs! They had a lot in common, even their desire for me. And though I never felt what everybody else felt when I smoked cocaine, Carlos and I quickly became friends and business partners in the drug game.

OVERDOSE

One day I was washing my clothes at Carlos's home, and he asked me if I were ready to "really" get high. I said yes. So he took the mirror off the dresser and taught me how to make base cocaine from raw cocaine powder. We cooked at least a half-ounce of cocaine, and then we went into the bathroom to hit it.

We didn't smoke from cans or hitters like drug addicts do today. We had cases of manufactured glass pipes that we got off the black market. Carlos told me to inhale or draw from the pipe as hard as I could, as he had already packed the head of the pipe with raw base cocaine.

> ON THE STREETS WE CALL THEM "FUNCTIONAL JUNKIES." THEY'RE STRUNG OUT, BUT THEY SOMEHOW MANAGE TO KEEP THEIR NINE-TO-FIVE JOBS.

When Carlos put the pipe to my mouth, all I remember is that I could not talk. Everything around me seemed to be moving as if a movie camera was spinning around on a tripod. When I finally spoke, my words were slurred and I didn't make any sense. My body responded as if I was having a stroke. It was my first "real" hit of base cocaine, and I had overdosed. I was finally high "for real."

I passed out, and Carlos laid me on his bed. He was stretching over me attempting to finally have his way sexually when, to his surprise, I woke up. With a frightened expression, I asked him, "Who are you?" He tried telling me he was Carlos, but my mind was so gone that I did not recognize him, and I screamed rape at the top of my voice. For some reason, in my mind, I thought an intruder had broken into my house to rape me. I did not even recognize I wasn't at home.

I wrestled with Carlos from the back of his house to the front door. He was always paranoid about the police, so he had several locks, chains, and bolts on the door. I was as strong as an ox and literally out of my mind. I grabbed him by the crotch of his pants and slammed him to the floor like we were part of the World Wrestling Federation.

I got to the last lock on the door and was about to run outside like a wild woman. Suddenly my mind came back, which must have been the hand of the Lord upon me. Relieved that I was returning to my *right* mind, Carlos dropped to his knees and said, "Thank You, Jesus," not even knowing the One he so adamantly gave thanks to.

If the police had stumbled on us that night, we would have been put away for a long time. Up until then, the closest I came to getting arrested was when I took a small package of cocaine to a drug dealer for him to snort while he was in jail. I drove to the police station located outside Gainesville, Florida, and my trunk was filled with ounces of dope and cases of drug paraphernalia. When I pulled my identification out, marijuana paper fell on the floor. That was probable cause to search me, and all they needed was a dog to sniff for the dope on my person.

There was no explanation for how I avoided going to jail for that incident except God spared me. Amazingly, I've never been arrested a day in my life. I give this testimony to the glory of God, because if anybody deserved to do jail time, I did.

"DOWN" ON A WHOLE NEW LEVEL

I wish I could report that I learned my lesson from my base cocaine overdose with Carlos and my narrow escape from being raped. Instead, I went to another level in abusing drugs. The demon that I allowed in my life now had control of me. Despite the awful experience of overdosing on base cocaine, at that time I would have given my life to feel it all again.

> NOTHING IS EVER LIKE THE FIRST "REAL" HIT, BECAUSE IT IS THE BAIT TO SNARE YOU. ONCE YOU'RE CAUGHT IN THE WEB OF ADDICTION, THE DEVIL DOES NOT OWE YOU ANYTHING. YOU'RE SIMPLY NOT A CHALLENGE TO HIM ANYMORE.

I had experienced what's called on the streets a "wallbanger." This means to reach the ultimate high. You only get one wallbanger in an addiction, and then you spend the rest of your time trying to obtain a feeling you will never feel again. Nothing is ever like the first "real" hit, because it is the bait to snare you. Once you're caught in the web of addiction, the devil does not owe you anything. You're simply not a challenge to him anymore. The devil enjoys the hunt! He roams around like a roaring lion seeking whom he can devour. Once he catches you, he chews on you for a while until you begin to rot, and then he moves on to his next victim.

CHAPTER 8

BACK WITH DANNY

D ANNY AND I did everything together, which is why I agreed to be with him despite his indiscretions with other women. I knew them all, but they did not know me. One young lady, in particular, was a model who had marble-colored eyes. They were so pretty that everyone called her "Green-eyes." She won the bathing suit contest at Florida A&M University, home to the most beautiful black women in the world.

Yes, Green-eyes was very conceited, but she loved the ground Danny walked on. In fact, he was the only one who could interrupt her world and make her think about someone other than herself.

The women in Danny's life didn't stop us from living together. A few days before we moved into our new place, we went on a two-week cocaine binge. One of Danny's friends told us Green-eyes was in town and that she had heard about me. His friend described her as "fire mad."

Somehow, I talked Danny into letting me pick her up to have a talk with her. Danny later told me he knew he had made a mistake after I drove off. When I met with Green-eyes, she told me how she was insulted that Danny would mess over her with somebody who looked like me. Miss Green-eyes was really full of herself.

She cussed me out and called me all kinds of names as I drove her to meet with Danny. My first intention was to take her to him. But the more she cussed, the more I sensed the spirit of Mrs. Ella Mae, my blind grandmother, speaking to me.

I could literally hear Big Momma's voice say, "Beat her down! Strike first! Ask questions later!"

Instead of taking Green-eyes to Danny as I had promised, I drove her to my apartment. She was about 5'11" with a cover-girl, Coca-Cola bottle shape, but my plan was to swell her up like a two-liter.

As the beauty queen entered my apartment, I made her think Danny was waiting for her. And then, out of nowhere, I struck her in the face without warning and commenced to beat her like I was a mad woman. She was much bigger than I was, and as I held her in a headlock, she bit a giant plug out of my left breast. Although I clearly got the best of her, my body was so sore that I later wondered if it all was worth it. As I was falling asleep that night, I told myself, "Yep, every minute of it!"

LIFE IN A CRACK HOUSE

For the first time in our relationship, Danny and I allowed our apartment to become a full-time crack house. My apartment was a place where all the junkies who bought drugs from us laid their head. There were Jamaicans, Haitians, Cubans, and others who came through the city with goods.

Though we were making a profit, I lived in constant fear and paranoia, because I was in over my head and things were moving too fast for me. One night there were dope dealers of every kind in the house comparing their products. They had manufactured pipes, scales, test tubes, and bottles of grain alcohol.

86

For some reason, I couldn't shake the thought of the vice squad kicking our door in. Every time I got high, I would imagine a newspaper headline flashing before me: "Track Star Busted for Cocaine." This was an unshakable fear. I had met my match—cocaine! Though I had broken many molds in my life, I couldn't break this one.

One night while watching dealers compare their dope, I began to hear the vice squad outside the door. They were cocking their weapons and giving each other signals. I knew I had to get out of that house, even if I had to leave Danny. Frantically, I begged Danny to help me get out.

As we drove down the street, police cars were surrounding us. I was so scared. I had the love of my life, Danny, drop me off at the home of a guy who we both knew liked me. When I came down off my trip and realized that the whole episode was only a nightmare, I started crying for the guy to take me back to Danny. I was losing my mind. There was no vice squad, no voices, no police cars, but it seemed so real. The demons were playing a game, and I was the joystick. The guy whose house Danny had taken me to looked at me and shook his head.

I can remember nights when Danny and I were so high, all we could do was lie in bed and hold each other while trembling. Our addictions were getting worse, and I could tell Danny needed more, something new. He needed help. But because I was a genuine junkie, I could not help him even though I wanted to.

As time went on, we started to experience manifestations of our addiction. For instance, when a person runs out of cocaine, a common reaction is to hallucinate. We actually thought we saw cocaine in the carpet or on the floor. Often, I would try to smoke pieces of soap, cotton, or anything that was white. I used to crawl on my knees for hours, collecting particles in hope that a rock had fallen from the pipe.

Another manifestation is to look out the window in paranoia. Although Danny usually acted pretty cool when he got high, I noticed that he was on the floor and at the window just like me. Who was going to look out for us now? We were both "geaking"! (*Geaking* is a term used in base houses. It means to see things that are not there.)

Cocaine had its hook in both of us. One night Danny got so high that he tried to hide from the police in the apartment pool. He was in the pool holding on to the sides with the water up to his neck. I was running around yelling at imaginary people who obviously weren't there. The merry-go-round of this horrible lifestyle was going faster, and we wanted to get off, but we were afraid to jump. After all, who would be there to catch us?

A MONKEY ON MY BACK

Other than Danny, I had literally cut myself off from everything and everybody. My goal in life was to get at least a quarter of an ounce to smoke a day. I could no longer get high off what I started out with.

No one wanted to get high with me. They said I would "blow their high," because I was a paranoid basket case. Everyone enjoyed smoking cocaine, but I took one hit and started hearing voices and even grabbing other peoples' cocaine and flushing it down the toilet.

As I think back, I thank God that I never got comfortable in the base house. I was really "out there" and had no idea how to come back in. I was a prophet out of place! Most of my friends who maintained their cool in the base house are still out there today!

One summer night, the voices I had always heard got so loud that I put my back against the front door and began to scream for the imaginary police to come and get me. When I saw tenants sleeping outside by the pool with sheets over them to ward off bugs, I ran to the pool area and snatched a sheet off of a tenant and yelled, "I knew you were out here!"

Embarrassed and frightened, I ran back to my spot at the window, holding my hands over my ears to stop the police from calling me out of the house. If I ever needed to be committed to a crazy house, it was then.

Some time later, Danny and I sat down to have a serious talk. He concluded that we could not continue to live the way we had done so. We were in jeopardy of being busted by the police—and not the imaginary police either. Another close accomplice had already been busted on the city bus.

Danny said we had to run, and I was willing to run anywhere with him. He explained to me that we had to go in separate directions. When he suddenly announced that he was leaving the next day, my breath left my body. I called my aunt Lillie Mae and begged her to tell him not to leave me. I told her I was on drugs and could not make it without him. I never cried so hard in my life.

Nothing I said was able to change Danny's course. He dropped me off at the same guy's house where I went the night I was paranoid. Danny drove off in a Chevrolet truck packed with his belongings, but I only had a bag of clothes. He left me on a Wednesday, and by Friday I was so sick I had to see a doctor. The doctor told me I was pregnant. This was a little comfort, because I felt like it might make a difference.

The next day I called Danny's grandfather and his exact words were, "He went to the wedding." It took me a while to catch on, and I had to ask him whose wedding it was. When he told me it was Danny's wedding, there was no need for me to attempt suicide, because I felt as if I died at that moment. For days I sat gazing at nothing, taking breaks only to cry. The only way I made it through the first week was by convincing myself that it was best for him to leave me; after all, I was just a "rock star."

BACK TO FRENCH TOWN

I moved around the corner from French Town, where I could easily walk to get a fix. At first I felt like I had nothing to lose. A big-time drug dealer named Frank was always after me, and he took me under his wing. He was always jealous of Danny, so he felt special sleeping with me, Danny's ex-old lady. He kept me high, put me in fancy hotels, bought me things, and promised to help me with Danny's baby. Since I had no concept of true royalty, all this made me fell like a queen. The crazy part is that I would often stay at his house with him and another girl who had babies from him. No one complained; it was real life in the dope game.

I was concerned about smoking cocaine while I was pregnant, but I knew another rock star who had smoked dope for nine months and her baby was very healthy. Every time I considered trying to quit during my pregnancy, the devil showed me how well her baby had turned out.

Frank got me an apartment, and I lived like a vampire—awake mostly during the night. If someone knocked on my door before noon, I thought they were crazy. My normal time for getting up was 3:00 p.m. I would eat a small meal at this time, and then hit the streets to set up something for the midnight hour. I used to refer to midnight as the witching hour. Everybody wanted to be settled into whatever dirt he or she was into by midnight.

After giving my heart to Jesus, I realized that from midnight to daybreak are important times to get on the wall of intercession. This is the time when many dope addicts are calling on God. They might not know Jesus at the time, but there are lots of prayers such as, "God, please let me come down this time, and I will never do it again." Every rock star prays this prayer.

The drugs began to take a toll on me, and my appearance started to decline. I was not gaining weight during my pregnancy. I started dressing without care. Colors did not matter. Bathing wasn't a priority. I began to take on the physical appearance of what I really was—a rock star. I still took pride in the fact that I was not a chicken head, which is the lowest a female junkie can be in the drug world.

Men would walk up to me and tell me how I *used* to look good. They would take the liberty to tell me how bad I looked at the time. When I ran to the mirror, the devil told me they were lying and that I still looked good. I found myself with men I could never have imagined being with. I insisted on maintaining a standard of what I would and would not do. And this was the only thing that separated me from the "chicken head" in my mind, but we were all prostitutes. I just chose *whom* I would do business with. A chicken head has no choice!

I eventually stopped crying over Danny though my heart became calloused and hard. I had no friends. I had seen supposed friends walk out on me, and I began to put my trust in no one.

ROCK BOTTOM

The demonic attacks I experienced while I was high increasingly got worse. I had not one associate, male or female. I only dealt with people for the purpose of getting a fix. One morning before daybreak, I ran upstairs to my neighbor's place to tell him someone was in my apartment. He looked at me as if he did not believe me. He would not let me in, nor would he come down to help me.

I went back to my apartment wondering why my neighbor had treated me so badly. The devil reminded me, "Nobody trusts a rock star. Everybody knows you are a junkie, and they won't believe a word you say. Besides, nobody is in the house anyway but you and me."

I knew I had hit rock bottom and that it was time to go back to Jacksonville. No one from home knew what I was going through. I called one of my saved friends and was crying as I told her about Danny leaving me, marrying someone else, and leaving me pregnant. To my shock, she and her sister burst out laughing at me. Though they did not actually say it, I could hear them thinking. *Not you, the track star, homecoming queen, and president of student council.*

How did you wind up here, going from "track star" to "crack star"? I was not even embarrassed, because the hurt went beyond shame. Another girlfriend and one of my old coaches picked up whatever was left of me and got me out of Tallahassee.

+ ——————— + ——————— +

AFTER GIVING MY HEART
TO JESUS, I REALIZED
THAT FROM MIDNIGHT
TO DAYBREAK ARE
IMPORTANT TIMES TO
GET ON THE WALL OF
INTERCESSION. THIS IS
THE TIME WHEN MANY
DOPE ADDICTS ARE
CALLING ON GOD. THEY
MIGHT NOT KNOW JESUS
AT THE TIME, BUT THERE
ARE LOTS OF PRAYERS...

+ ——————— + ——————— +

I moved home and visited uptown daily. I could tell that things were getting worse on the streets. Once, when a drunken old man called me a name, my brother, Elliot, savagely attacked and beat him until he was bloody. I begged him to stop and had to pull him off the man who had put up no resistance at all.

My brother kicked him one last time and, cursing, said, "This old man lives by the laws of the streets. He didn't have to be here, but as long as he chooses to be here, he has to suffer the consequences!" It was a few years after this that my brother was gunned down with six bullets, two blocks away from where he beat the old man. When you live by the laws of the streets, you will surely die by them one day.

IN THE ARMY

After six months of separation, I finally talked with Danny on the telephone. I did not discuss my baby or his marriage. I later found out that his so-called friends told him I was not pregnant, that I was just tripping as usual. People had told him lies, claiming that I was only pretending.

After talking with Danny, I hung up the phone like it was a wrong number and then hit the streets. If it hurt, I did not let myself feel it. My motto with men was that I would not "love hard" anymore! I suppressed the love I had for him and chose not to meditate on the memories of our happy times together. I had to move on with my life, but somehow things were moving a little too fast.

One day I got in a conflict with a dangerous guy in uptown. I borrowed a pistol and went back on the street threatening to kill him. The look in my eyes let him know that I meant business. I embarrassed him in front of all his friends, and I knew I had to make a move. It was in me to kill, and I knew I had to make some changes in my life.

I ran to the army recruiting office and told them I needed the first assignment they had. Within a few days, I was at the reception station on orders to go to basic training. Grace had run out for me on the streets, and I knew it. Something told me that if I stayed on the streets, I would not survive long. I did not know God then, but a voice told me to run to the army. I know now that *someone* was not the devil!

CHAPTER 9

THE ARMY LIFE

My transition from the streets to the military is quite a story. The army recruiter picked me up from the base house. I was freebasing while peeping out the window when he arrived for me. The recruiter waited in the car as I took my last hit. I was shocked when I arrived at the transfer center and found out I had to take a urinalysis!

I thought to myself, *I'm going to burn these bottles up!* When I went into the latrine, I saw a vision that seemed too good to be true. I saw bottles of urine just sitting on the counter! This was too easy. I quickly placed my urine in a bottle and switched it with another bottle on the counter.

I know what you are thinking; some poor girl did not get into the military because of my dishonesty. It was life or death for me, and I had to get into the army. I pray for that young lady and believe God compensated her for what happened. Enlisting in the military was a part of my destiny, and I felt at the time that it had to be done.

My eight weeks of basic training changed my life. The number eight in the Bible is considered the number for new beginnings, and truly, I needed to try something new.

When I stepped on the cattle truck, I could not even spell the word *discipline*. It is amazing how God will use natural tools to make a spiritual difference in our lives. I could not relate to the spiritual, so God used the military to put me on the right track.

The drill sergeants scared the life out of most of the women in my group. To me they all looked like a group of squares. I had no respect for their authority, and they knew it. The first day, the head drill sergeant walked up to me and said, "Private, you think you're bad, but I'm gonna break you!" All I could think was that if what I had already been through could not break me, he wouldn't be able to either.

To make matters worse, I had a bad reputation in the platoon. I got in trouble every other day for fighting someone in the bathroom, mostly beating up white girls. I would catch them and slap them around. And no matter how much I threatened them, they still snitched on me.

As a result, I was in the drill sergeant's office every day. He'd say, "Private Parrish, drop! Get up! Get down!" The more they tried to punish my body, the stronger I got. They could not break me with physical punishment because as a track and field athlete, I was physically fit. Even straight from the crack house, I could outrun every woman in the platoon. The drill sergeants would get in our faces, nose to nose, and curse us out. I walked away from them smiling, because they didn't have anything on how my grandmother would talk to me.

THE BREAKING GROUND

Drill sergeants are trained to mess with your mind, but I had just come out of the devil's basic training—the base house! If Scorpion, Killer, and Razor couldn't break me on the streets, my drill sergeant didn't have a chance.

My immediate drill sergeant hated my guts. This was not just a part of a game played with every recruit—he really had a problem with me. He called me nappy head, told me my breath stunk, and cursed me like a sailor. One day I rolled my eyes at him, and the two of us went chest-to-chest cursing each other out. He gave me permission to tell him what was on my mind, and I gave it to him Grandma-Ella-Mae style.

Halfway through my training, I got tendonitis in my left ankle. They put a cast on my leg up to my knee. I never ran for physical training during my entire eight weeks, so I stayed in the barracks and slept, which was unheard of. None of the women asked me to clean any of the common areas, because my grandmother's belligerent nature would rise up in me and I would want to curse and fight. They just left me alone rather than deal with my demons.

Throughout the battalion I earned the reputation as the soldier who would not break. So wherever I went, the drill sergeants tried to gang up on me. They would put me on the wall and search me like they were the police. When I got the cast on my leg, they couldn't make me do push-ups, so they made me stand on one leg while holding my M-16 in the air. That meant lifting my heavy cast leg.

KP (kitchen police) was a place for people who got into trouble, but I felt like I was part of the permanent staff. I washed so many dishes I couldn't keep count of them. Drill sergeants constantly harassed me. A group of them would see me from a distance and yell, "Halt! Get up against the wall!" Almost every day, they threatened to send me to jail, but somehow it never happened.

I remember one time when the platoon went to spend three days in the woods, and I got into major trouble. We slept in tents that were only large enough for two people to lie side by side. I am not a wilderness sister, so I slept with my sleeping bag zipped up to my face. Sometime during the night, I felt something like a snake crawl across my sleeping bag. To this day, I do not know if it was my imagination or not.

The number one rule in the woods is never leave your buddy.

Well, I left my buddy and found my way through the woods to the large, warm tent where all the drill sergeants slept. I cuddled on the floor in the back of their tent and slept like a baby.

The next morning, I was awakened by ten angry drill sergeants yelling over me. They cursed me out and declared that I was the craziest trainee they had ever seen!

Two weeks before graduation, my favorite drill sergeant sarcastically reminded me that because of my cast, I would never be able to pass the physical required to get out of basic training. I would have to be "recycled." I thought I would get out of basic training, but now it looked like I would be locked down for eight more weeks.

Just when I thought I'd have to spend more time training, a nice drill sergeant caught me sleeping while on guard duty. As he walked around with me to check the bunks, he gave me a helpful suggestion. He told me that if my cast slipped off while I was taking a shower, I could try to pass my physical fitness test.

At first I couldn't understand what he was suggesting, because I couldn't figure out how my cast would slip off my leg in the shower. When I still didn't get the point, he said, "Cut the cast off and take your physical fitness test, private."

I followed his instructions and scored a perfect three hundred points on my test. After that, I started treating people better and even helped my bunkmates with the chores. Something was happening to me, and I found myself wanting to be a part of what was going on. Something broke in me; I did not want to be recycled.

The senior drill sergeant called me into his office and told me I had been a sharp soldier for the past two weeks. He even apologized to me, saying he should have made me squad or platoon leader. His theory was that I would have been more open to his training, and the women under me would have been well supervised.

He spoke words that I could not believe: "You are a born leader!" He was a white man, and up until a few weeks ago, he was an enemy. The words he spoke let me know that I was going to make it in the army after all. I just needed to hear somebody in authority tell me so. I graduated from basic training and went to advance training with a new attitude. I still had a lot to learn about following orders, but I was willing. The principles in the Bible are true whether we know them or not, and God was teaching me an important truth: "If you are willing and obedient, you shall eat of the good of the land" (Isa. 1:19).

ADVANCE TRAINING

I arrived at advance training with a newfound freedom, but they did have a few restrictions for new soldiers. I broke the rules the first day. I sneaked off post with the first guy who asked to take me out. My drill sergeant caught me in the act. After only two days I was on extra detail duty. My drill sergeant was called the "heart buster," because he was the meanest guy on post.

I was cleaning his office for extra duty, and he asked, "Soldier, when are you going to do right?" He said that if I followed the rules I could go out on a date like everyone else. I stopped sweeping the floor, walked over to his desk, and told him that I did not want to go out until he took me out.

His eyes seemed to pop out of his head. Sergeant Al was forty-five, and I was twenty-seven. I smiled at him and went to my room. I was off restriction the next day, and my advance training was a breeze from that day forward. He was married with children, but that did not matter to me. He became my boyfriend, and I ran the entire platoon through him. There were times he would have me on the balcony pretending to scold me, while he was telling me where to meet him that night.

When I graduated from my advance training, Al personally drove me to Florida and met my parents. His plans were to meet me in Germany at my first duty station, but he was killed during an argument with another soldier.

BACK ON TRACK

My first duty station was in Germany. I learned as much as I could about the military, but after hours I hung out in the party scene. When I met with the company commander for my first interview, he asked me what my goals were while overseas. Before I could even think about it, I blurted out, "Sir, I'm gonna be the fastest female military sprinter in Europe!" I felt like I was in the mold-breaking business again.

I started sending money home to my son. I became a good steward in saving money so my child could join me. This time, not only did I get a car, but I purchased a Mercedes. I was back on the right track.

> WITHIN A YEAR, I WAS NOT ONLY THE FASTEST FEMALE IN EUROPE, BUT I WAS ALSO THE FASTEST IN THE ENTIRE MILITARY. MY ALL-ARMY TRACK STATUS FOLLOWED ME EVERYWHERE I WENT.

Within a year, I was not only the fastest female in Europe, but I was also the fastest in the entire military. My all-army track status followed me everywhere I went. I always got easy duty assignments that would allow me time to train. I got to know the Department of the Army Athletic Staff, and they kept close watch on my off-season activities. I took pride in being a sharp soldier and made sure I met the requirements for a promotion.

Within four years I became a staff sergeant (E-6) in the United States Army. Normally it took eight years to make this type of rank at the time. I did not know the Lord, but He knew me before I was formed in my mother's womb. He knew me in the base house, and He knew me on the winner's podium. I'm glad that when I did not even take time to tell Him "thank You" for waking me up in the morning, He looked past my faults and saw my needs.

My single years overseas were my party years, and I dated a lot of guys. I even agreed to marry guys and left them standing at the altar. After Danny left me, my life's motto was, "I do not love hard anymore!"

After returning to the United States, Mike-Mike finally moved back with me. I was stationed at Ft. Stewart, Georgia, and Hunter Army Airfield. I was financially stable and could provide for him like I never imagined. I purchased my first home, paid off my first car, and kept money in the bank and in my pocket. By the fifth of each month, every bill was paid. Mike-Mike lived like children I had only seen on television.

The club scene got old, and I had so many boyfriends for the first five years of the military that I can't name them all. I had some good friends, but I loved all of them the same—cautiously! I did not have a lot of boyfriends at any one time, but my turnover rate was high. If a guy rubbed me the wrong way, I simply went on to the next phase, a new man.

FINALLY MARRIED?

Danny visited me in Georgia. He seemed to be successful in life, and I was happy for him. I spent the day and all night with him. I was excited to show him around the army installation, because I wanted him to know that I was doing well.

Danny was still my friend, and I did not hate him. I had forgiven him, but something in me would not allow me to forgive myself. I felt as if what had happened between us was my fault. I was a dope head. If I could have been straight, I could have helped him.

Deep inside, I knew Danny had done the right thing by marrying. His wife had a decent life and had so much to offer, or so I thought! Spending the day with Danny did not spark an old fire;

101

I couldn't let it happen. My rule of thumb stood for him, too. I did not love hard anymore, not even Danny! If I still loved him, I couldn't tell it! I knew he belonged to someone else, and I had hoped he was happy. My emotions were unmoved, but I still knew he was my best friend.

But there was a young man who I took an interest in, and we got married. We seemed to get along, and he was good for Mike. One reason I got married was my son, Mike-Mike, needed a father figure in his life. I was really tired of the dating game, and I wanted to settle down with a decent fellow. The day I got married I almost missed the ceremony. I was standing in the grocery store line at 5:15 p.m., when Mike-Mike reminded me I was getting married at 5:30. My husband-to-be was dressed in a nice suit, but I wore a pair of old jeans because I did not have time to change. We had been shacking together for a year, so the ceremony was only a formality to me.

As we approached the judge, I reminded my soon-to-be-husband that I did believe in divorce if our marriage didn't work out. In my mind the ceremony was a "swearing in." What a vow!

Circumstances had rushed our decision to get married. We were living together, and I received orders to go back to Germany. We

> "GOD WANTS TO USE YOUR HOUSE TO SHELTER AND FEED THE HOMELESS." I THOUGHT, *GOD CAN USE IT FOR WHATEVER HE WANTS TO USE IT FOR, AS LONG AS HE CAN PAY IT OFF!* ALTHOUGH THE MAN KEPT SAYING, "THIS IS THE HOUSE!" HE RODE HIS OLD BIKE DOWN THE ROAD, NEVER TO BE SEEN AGAIN.

had to make a quick decision to separate or to get married. I was faced with an either-or situation, and I took the easiest way out—I thought.

I was on orders for Germany, and the Lord started to get my attention. There was a saved woman who lived in my neighborhood, but she never had food to feed her children. She would come over and say, "Well, I guess I'll put my children to bed without dinner." I did not know anything about being saved, but I figured if being saved meant I had to starve, I did not want to be a Christian. I would pack bags of groceries and feed the woman and her children. I did not try to figure it out.

During this time in my life, I was having nightmares all the time. It happened whenever Mike and I were home alone. I would see little imps pulling him out of my bed, and when I got up to check on him, he would be sleepwalking. These recurring dreams were so real that I would often make him sleep with me so I could put one arm around him and hold him.

One night as I was walking from my room to his, I saw hundreds of the little imps having orgies on my floor. I had to step over them to get to Mike's room. I never told anyone, because I already had a record at the crazy house and did not want to add to it.

"FOR SALE" AND REDEEMED

On a beautiful spring day, an old man came to my house, because I had placed a For Sale sign in the yard. He told me he was interested in buying my house. And as he walked inside, he said God was telling him, "This is the house!" I was following the man with my legal papers so we could talk business, but he was just walking and praying in a strange language.

Finally he said, "God wants to use your house to shelter and feed the homeless."

I thought, *God can use it for whatever He wants to use it for, as long as He can pay it off!* Although the man kept saying, "This is the house!" he rode his old bike down the road, never to be seen again. It really did not make sense to use my house as a shelter for the homeless anyway; it was in the middle of a residential neighborhood.

I never thought twice about this strange visitation, but six months later my entire household was saved. It was not until years later that I realized it was not a physical house that God wanted, but He wanted my physical being to minister to the desolate. I thank God that He chose my house that day.

My conversion was initiated by watching a movie called *A Thief in the Night*. This movie rocked my world, and I wasn't good for anything but Jesus. I found out that I was on my way to hell and urgently needed a change in course. The first thing I thought about was my friend who laughed at me when I told her Danny left me. She had led me in the sinner's prayer at that time, but I had forgotten all about it. I am so glad Jesus did not forget.

I went to Germany a new creature in Christ Jesus, but I was in much need of deliverance. When I arrived at my duty station, Allah, Jehovah, and the Mormons were all waiting on me. I went to Frankfurt, Germany, this time, and every kind of cult leader approached me. I thought it was funny that when I was a heathen, they did not bother me. Now that I had accepted Jesus, the battle was on for the truth. The good thing was that I took Mike overseas with me.

I will never forget boarding the airplane after we had watched *A Thief in the Night*. I told Mike that I was going to give my life to the Lord. He told me, "Mom, you're too late; I have already accepted Jesus in my life!"

CHAPTER 10

A BABE IN CHRIST

I DID NOT UNDERSTAND a lot about the Christian life, but I knew Jesus was the only One who gave me peace. For the first time, I did not have to depend on my skills and abilities. I had found Someone who loved me unconditionally just as I was.

Becoming a part of a church, however, was a different story. I tried attending a holiness church, but they politely asked me to leave because of the way I looked. They were not use to seeing a Christian with gold teeth and wearing provocative street clothing.

God delivered me from drugs, profanity, fighting, and other sinful behavior like a bolt of lightning. But some things, like the way I dressed or my worldly mannerisms, came off in layers. Although I was saved, I still had a strong, worldly flavor in my life, especially in how I dressed.

I had never been one to give up, so I tried another church in the same denomination. I was so glad to be saved, and I wanted the world to know that Jesus was Lord of my life. The church service went well. Some of the sisters invited me over for dinner; however, they told me to bring a change of clothes.

LOOKING SAVED BUT NOT SANCTIFIED

I decided that I wanted to look *really* saved when I had dinner with the sisters, so I wore a pair of lo-o-o-ong shorts. The shorts reached my knees, but were still very tight. (Hey, this was a leaps-and-bounds improvement for me. My usual summer attire would have given them a heart attack.) I was trying so hard to fit in, and judging from where I had come from, I was doing fine.

We have to be very careful not to judge people based on appearance. If those women had discerned my heart, they would have realized I was a work in progress. The process of sanctification is ongoing in the believer's life. We have no idea what the Lord has delivered sinners from. Our hang-ups and idiosyncrasies can tear down the work God has begun in them.

> GOD DELIVERED ME FROM DRUGS, PROFANITY, FIGHTING, AND OTHER SINFUL BEHAVIOR LIKE A BOLT OF LIGHTNING. BUT SOME THINGS, LIKE THE WAY I DRESSED OR MY WORLDLY MANNERISMS, CAME OFF IN LAYERS.

My hair was cut in a punk-rock style with a variety of different colors. I felt as if my hairstyle was all right, but apparently the sisters didn't agree. Whenever I sat down next to one of them at dinner, they immediately moved. They treated me so badly that I began to sniff my underarms to see if I stunk. They thought they looked so holy, but I could see straight through them.

I went to the sister who invited me to church and asked her if

I should leave. With sorrow in her eyes, she said it might be best for me to go. After she quickly walked away and left me standing alone, I got my things and escorted myself to the door. Not only did they neglect to feed me, but no one even showed me how to get home. I was in a small town in a foreign country, and I was unfamiliar with the area.

I cried all the way home, praying that God would lead me home safely. Hungry and lost in a foreign country, I felt like a foreigner in the body of Christ. I had never been a churchgoer, so there was much I did not know. I had to depend on God for everything. Nothing I knew from my previous life applied to the spiritual realm, because my former life was based on worldly and fleshly things. Like a new baby, I had to learn everything all over again.

TURNED ON TO JESUS

The simplest things in God were so important to me. I had something inside me that every born-again believer should have—a desire to know the whole truth. In the world I liked my cocaine raw. Cocaine used to be "my thang." It turned me on. Now Jesus is "my thang," because He turns me on. I do not want another spirit, something that would adulterate or water down the truth. I like my God "raw," and I refuse to settle for anything less.

This is important, because only the truth will make us free. As part of the End-Time remnant of God, we don't have time for frivolous distractions and hindrances. The ultimate purpose of adulteration of the truth is to mix it with leaven. The Bible says a little leaven will leaven the whole truth!

I was walking around in my living room in Frankfurt one day, and I heard a voice say clearly, "Beware of the leaven of the Sadducees and Pharisees." Once I got a revelation that God did not want me to be religious, I held on to it with everything in my heart. I got it! I understood what God was saying, and I needed to beware.

A little hypocrisy could spoil the call of God on my life! A little pride could leave me void of any miracles, and a little haughtiness could quench the anointing on my life!

> WE HAVE TO BE VERY CAREFUL NOT TO JUDGE PEOPLE BASED ON APPEARANCE. IF THOSE WOMEN HAD DISCERNED MY HEART, THEY WOULD HAVE REALIZED I WAS A WORK IN PROGRESS. THE PROCESS OF SANCTIFICATION IS ONGOING IN THE BELIEVER'S LIFE. WE HAVE NO IDEA WHAT THE LORD HAS DELIVERED SINNERS FROM. OUR HANG-UPS AND IDIOSYNCRASIES CAN TEAR DOWN THE WORK GOD HAS BEGUN IN THEM.

I was living for Jesus the best I knew when I received orders to return to Presidio, California, to train for track season. I even received a special bonus. I had been chosen to be the sprint coach. In years past, I was the fastest woman in all four armed forces, but my contentious attitude had earned me a reputation. Not a season went by without me cursing someone out. For instance, one year I picked up a pair of heavy starting blocks and began swinging them at a 220-pound male athlete.

The major who was in charge of overseeing the team had overlooked these incidents and only punished me with room restriction. I was allowed to leave my room for track practice, and there were times when my roommates had to bring my meals to me. I behaved this way for years. They put up with my fits because I could win the gold. But this time I was going for training as a whole new woman.

A New Woman

In 1988, I boarded the plane for training camp, but for the first time in my life Jesus was leading the way. The first team meeting was very dramatic for me. For years I had lived like a heathen, and now I had to tell all the athletes I was saved. We usually picked on all the so-called "saved" athletes. How would the team accept me now?

I stood up to announce that the air force had recruited a group of college athletes. I explained to them that we had a great challenge for the upcoming season. I closed my speech by saying, "Through Christ Jesus, we can do all things!" The bus was silent. Many looked around to make sure what they heard was right.

Many of the athletes shook their heads in disbelief and said they would believe it when they saw it in my life. They were not willing to believe I was saved—I had to *show* them!

After a few weeks, everybody knew my conversion was legitimate. Still, they watched me like a hawk. They waited and listened for foul language to spew out of my mouth. People even tried to instigate fights by starting arguments with me. In no time, 50 percent of the team was saved. We met to pray at 7:00 p.m. every night in the basement. We knew nothing about the Bible, so everyone took turns reading a verse, and then we prayed prayers that I knew touched the heart of God.

We spent several weeks looking for a church, but from what we could tell, Jesus was not in any of the churches we visited. We went to several denominations "looking for Jesus," but it seemed that we were looking for love (and Jesus) in all the wrong places. Even when we went to the big cathedrals, we could not find Him there.

The last girl to get saved was a javelin thrower, and she told us she had found a church that Jesus was in. It was a small church that had a seating capacity for no more than seventy-five to eighty people.

The pastor was in his mid-twenties, but a female evangelist was speaking when we visited. She prophesied that there were three young women in the congregation whom God was calling to the fivefold ministry. Nothing in me said that I was one of the girls, so I looked around to see who it could be. My natural mind could not fathom God using a person like me.

SHADOWED BY THE DEVIL

The closer I got to God, the more opposition I felt. I could not put my finger on it, but I felt as if somebody or something was following me around. One day, instead of leading my team to church I told them to go alone. I went to the club, played bingo, drank alcohol, and smoked a cigarette. What was happening to me? I had no control of the decision-making process. Not even the unsaved Kim would have gone to the club a few days before the big meet.

It was as though some force was leading my steps, and before long, the devil personally introduced himself to me. I had promised the javelin thrower I would buy her a dress for church when she got saved. But to my surprise, when my pay stub came it said, "No pay due."

How was I going to live? My son was in Germany living with a family while I trained. I began to feel heavy about the situation, and I fell asleep feeling hopeless. Yet as I slept, Jesus hovered above me. He told me He loved me and that He would take care of me. Jesus then wrapped me in His arms and told me everything would be all right.

The Lord talked with me much of the night, and then I had a dream. I saw a woman with a big check standing in the financial aid office. The check was huge, and it had my name written on it in bold print.

When I woke up from the dream, I realized I was late for a finance appointment I had scheduled earlier. The financial aid office was in the building next to my barracks, and as I ran through the office door I was shocked to see the woman in my dream standing in the office.

When I told the woman my name, she said she had a check for me! When I walked out the door with the check in my hand, I realized it was not even payday. The military sometimes would issue pay statements before the money was actually distributed. The devil was telling me I would not get paid, but God had paid me early.

LESSONS ABOUT FAITH

For the first six months of my Christian life, and paying my tithes, I had to fight for my paycheck every month. It is quite ironic for a military person to have to worry about a check. But now I know the military has a ruler spirit presiding over it. The spirit tries to present itself as your provider. It assures you of what we called "three hots and a cot." This meant three meals a day and a place to lay your head at night.

In my case, though, my check was being garnished for a debt I incurred before yoking up with Uncle Sam. As I traveled around the world in the military, every payday told the same story: "No pay due." Those in the finance office would tell me there was nothing they could do for me and would ask me to leave. Nevertheless, I sat quietly in my chair, praying in tongues under my breath and reading Kenneth Hagin's books on faith. For six months, despite how crazy people thought I was, I never argued and never left without full pay.

I will never forget the day God delivered me from this situation. I walked into the finance office in Fort Stewart, Georgia. The officer recognized me and said, "You can flip on your head today. But you have no check due, and you will not get one." I sat down and began to read my books and pray as usual. One of my friends came in and tried to convince me that I was making a fool of myself. She encouraged me to get a loan from the Army Emergency Relief. I told her that as a tither and a child of the King, I would accept nothing less than what God said I could have.

The Lord had instructed me how to walk through this dry season, but every devil in hell was on the scene to ensure that I would not pass the test. Five minutes before the office closed for the day, the phone rang, and a lady on the other end said she was calling in reference to Kimberly Parrish's case. I heard the finance officer say in amazement, "She is in our office now!" The lady asked to speak with me. When I put my ear to the phone, she said words that shook my very soul: "Jesus is Lord!"

The woman was calling from the Department of the Army Finance Office in Virginia. She said the Lord had been dealing with her concerning my situation. She explained that the debt had been forgiven, and I would not have to deal with the situation anymore. Hallelujah! I passed the test!

If we pass the tests we go through in life, it will be just as God told Israel: the enemies we see today, we shall see no more (Exod. 14:13). When I received my LES (Leave and Earnings Statement), my heart rejoiced as I saw typed on a Department of the Army form: "Debt forgiven." Jesus is Lord!

I still have that paper today. Every now and then I look at it to remind me of my tailor-made miracle from God. What God has for me is for me! The devil is not the only one who has people strategically positioned in high places. To God be the glory!

CHAPTER 11

TIMES OF TESTING

T HE BIBLE SAYS the enemy comes immediately to steal the word that has been sown in our hearts. The devil clearly did not like my new faith and endurance in God. He could not make me bow with a natural challenge such as financial distress, so he came at me with a spirit of witchcraft.

One of the other coaches hated me and wanted nothing to do with God. When I lived for the devil, he practically kissed the ground I walked on. But when I sold out to Jesus, he despised my very presence. As I would lead athletes to the Lord and pray for them, like a wolf, the devil tried to devour them at inception.

This particular coach had never been a good athlete. When I was a recruit and on the track team, he would always get cut from the team and sent back to his unit. He definitely wasn't a good coach either, but somehow he convinced the Department of the Army to give him a break. He was a "yes sir" boy and seemed to just be filling a slot so someone else could run the team through him.

You have to be watchful of people who want what you have. This man was ruled by a spirit of failure and was jealous of my leadership ability and my gift of being a champion. The spirit of failure worked with rejection and insecurity to lead him headfirst into rebellion. The spirit of jealousy and coveting are obsessive spirits and will make people cross spiritual lines.

This is the sort of mind-set that motivates mass murderers and serial killers. Their obsession starts with thoughts such as: *Since no one is paying any attention to me, I will kill as many people as I can. Then they will pay attention to me!* A person with this type of personality can entertain demons for selfish motives and be quickly escorted into the realm of the demonic.

Witchcraft is amazingly subtle at its inception in a human being. It is deceptive in nature and operates best behind closed doors. Witchcraft is able to flourish, because people respond to it with ignorance. The word *ignorance* simply means "a lack of knowledge." God says in His Word people perish because they lack knowledge (Hos. 4:6). To *perish* means "to be ruined or destroyed." We have many casualties in the body of Christ due to ignorance.

Proverbs 1:29 gives a description of people who hate knowledge and who don't choose the fear of the Lord. Psalm 25:14 says the secret of the Lord is with those who fear Him. Those who fear God know witchcraft is God's enemy. Satan is the god of this world, and to be a friend of the world is to be a friend of the devil. He is the god of witchcraft.

THE MIDNIGHT HOUR

I went to bed early one night and was awakened at 3:00 a.m. by a sharp pain in my side. Because of the intensity of my workouts, I rarely got up before 5:30 a.m. I went to the bathroom, but as I walked the pain grew more intense.

Although I did not understand anything concerning witchcraft at that time in my Christian life, I knew something was wrong with me, and I knew it was not natural. Something supernatural was going on, but at first I had no idea what it was.

Bent over and in pain, I happened to pass by the door of a young man who hated me. With a smirk on his face, he stood at the door and looked at me, never even asking what was wrong. By this time I was yelling at the top of my voice for someone to get me to the hospital. I felt like I was in labor, but the pain was even more severe than labor.

At the emergency room I screamed for about an hour, begging my roommate to do something to help me. I could see her compassion, but she felt helpless. She couldn't ease my suffering. My roommate was the only young lady who had not given her life to Jesus, but her mother was a praying woman. My roommate gently placed her hand on my head and simply said, "In the name of Jesus."

The doctor had taken tests, and he called me into his office to give me an evil report about my condition. But before he could drop the bomb on me, he wanted to run more tests. Praise God, the next set of tests were negative. The doctor would not tell me his first finding, because he said the first X-rays weren't mine!

There was no way two X-rays could look so different. One X-ray was cursed and the other was blessed. I quickly learned that Satan could not curse whom God had blessed. This drew much attention, but the medical staff cited human error rather than give God the glory for another miracle.

I asked my roommate why she laid hands on me, and she did not even understand why she had done it. I learned that God will take the foolish to confound the wise, and there is a way that seems right to a man but the end of it is death.

Years later it all made sense to me. I happened to be living in San Francisco, which was one of the satanic capitals of the world. In fact, San Francisco was home to the Church of Satan at the time. In addition to being attacked by witchcraft, I was also vulnerable to demonic influences, because I was not totally delivered from the consequences of past sins.

QUALIFYING FOR THE OLYMPIC TRIALS

I was taking anabolic steroids for the first time. Another female athlete, who was a world-class competitor, took me to what's called a "head shop." Now I know it's a store that sells artifacts for witchcraft. I walked in for a minute, but I couldn't stay inside. This store sold satanic bibles and all kinds of other creepy items.

At the time I never wondered why she would go into a place like that. Later God revealed to me that she was not only on anabolic steroids like I was, but she was also praying to Satan asking for supernatural athletic ability.

I definitely had no interest in serving the devil, but I was very ignorant about the many ways he can get a foothold in a new believer's life. I was so ignorant of the dark side that I took frequent trips to Chinese shops for acupuncture. Even the wildest athletes knew something was wrong with acupuncture. I wanted healthy legs, and I would have done anything short of serving the devil to get them.

In New Mexico in 1988, I had already qualified for the Olympic Trials. I was winning the final race of the 100-meter when I pulled a muscle ten yards before the finish line.

What I did not know was that, in fact, I was serving Satan by participating in demonic practices. After the attack on my body, I was healed and ready to run track again. The air force, marines, and navy came to Presidio that year to compete. The night before the meet, God spoke strongly and told me to leave San Francisco. I could hear Him clearly bidding me to leave. In the natural it sounded crazy, but somehow I felt I was not dealing with a natural situation.

I got my roommate up and explained to her that I had to leave.

She thought I was crazy. It was so difficult walking away from track and field at the peak of my career.

DEALING WITH THE DEVIL

I went home on leave for a few days and stayed with Perk and my stepmom, Ruth. She was saved and filled with the Holy Ghost, even though she and my father were living together. All I could see was how she had changed. In the past we used to smoke dope together and hang out at the sissy show. Seeing the change in her lifestyle impacted my life.

One day, my stepmother casually mentioned they had cast demons out of a woman at her church. After hearing that, I followed her around all day, begging her to tell me demons weren't real. I thought if demons were real, then all my dreams about demons and Mike-Mike were not dreams after all.

Despite my efforts to dissuade her, my stepmother wouldn't back down from her belief in the reality of demons. But it was all coming together for me. The attack on my body, the voices in the crack house, and the little imps that pulled Mike-Mike from the bed were all demons. At that moment, I decided the devil would not torment me anymore. I decided to retaliate.

I flew back to my duty station, and the devil was waiting on me at the airport. It seemed as if a dark cloud was following me around. I could literally sense an evil presence.

When I arrived at the military installation, I tried to hang out with the "saved" girls, but it did not work. There was something about them that kept me from getting close to them. Admittedly, I was still smoking, and a curse word would slip out every now and then.

I asked them what was the difference between them and me. They replied, "We have the Holy Ghost." I asked them how did they know they were filled with the Holy Ghost. Their response was so shallow that I knew they were only mimicking what they had heard or read. I needed the whole truth, and they didn't seem to have it. I badgered them about having something so real, but yet they couldn't explain it to me.

I had only been on normal duty for two weeks when my step-mother called and said she was attending Kenneth Hagin's Camp Meeting in a few days. At the time, I carried a case of Kenneth Hagin books with me everywhere I went. Every spare moment, I was studying his Bible teachings. It took a lot of self-control not to read at red traffic lights while I was driving, but I knew I wanted whatever this Hagin guy had.

I told my stepmother I would see her at the Hagin meetings, and she told me she thought I was crazy. Most people planned all year for the trip, and she didn't think I could jump on the boat at the last minute. What she did not understand was that I *had* to get there. All of my circumstances said no, but something inside me insisted yes.

I had negative twenty-one days of leave available, meaning I actually owed the army twenty-one days. Yet, my first sergeant approved me for an additional twenty days. That was God! I had been back in the country for three days from ninety days of all-army training and leave when God supernaturally paid for my plane ticket through the army. Plus, the twenty-day leave never showed up on my pay stubs, neither was the cost of the plane ticket deducted. The Holy Ghost had given me a free trip to go and get delivered.

Despite the blessings of God, the demonic opposition got stronger. A few days before leaving for camp meeting, while I was asleep, long, hairy monkey arms started coming from under all four sides of the bed. These arms began strapping me down. As I called on Jesus, I heard a voice yell, "Shut up!" and one of the arms covered my mouth.

Even though my flesh was still pinned to the bed, my spirit man took over and continued calling on Jesus. As the battle raged, the lights in my house began flickering on and off. The devil didn't bother me so much when I first got saved, but he waged an all-out attack when I began seeking God for the baptism in the Holy Spirit and for deliverance.

I will never forget the fear that came over me in my apartment that day in Frankfurt. Mike-Mike was visiting in the States, and I was living alone and afraid. I started sleeping on the floor of my soldiers' barracks. But I told the other Christian girls I had met on post that when I returned from the United States, I would be speaking in tongues and sleeping in my own bed. But still, it was a battle every step of the way.

The BMW I was driving to the airport in Germany broke down. Running out of time to catch my plane, I had to hitchhike to the airport. When I sent someone to pick up the car along the road and have it towed for service, it worked fine for that person. When I arrived in the States, I had a Mercedes to ride in—but it broke down, too!

> AS THE BATTLE RAGED, THE LIGHTS IN MY HOUSE BEGAN FLICKERING ON AND OFF. THE DEVIL DIDN'T BOTHER ME SO MUCH WHEN I FIRST GOT SAVED, BUT HE WAGED AN ALL-OUT ATTACK WHEN I BEGAN SEEKING GOD FOR THE BAPTISM IN THE HOLY SPIRIT AND FOR DELIVERANCE.

Clearly the Lord was planning something special for me at the camp meeting, and the devil was doing everything he could to prevent it from happening.

CHAPTER 12

FREE INDEED

∞

I MADE IT TO camp meeting, and it was awesome. I had never seen anything like it. After the first night I was tired from jet lag and wanted to go to bed, but my roommate told me they were having prayer on the eighth floor. As I put on my pajamas, I heard a voice say, "Go." I went to the prayer meeting with a young lady from Jacksonville whom I had met on the trip.

Something in me was afraid to go in that room, but I felt safe with this new friend. When I walked into the room, I felt God's presence like never before. What was this unusual prayer language? They would even sing in this language, and they sounded like one voice. I knew one thing; I had to have this language!

These people were Baptists, and even new believers know that Baptists don't pray in tongues. But God said that in the last days He would pour out His Spirit on all flesh. That included the Baptists and even me. Others who had traveled from Florida with me were attempting to get me filled with the Holy Ghost. Every time they laid hands on me, the demons would choke me and make me fall out. But something was different in the room I was in. I had never felt this way before.

A young man came into the room and started speaking in tongues and then interpreted, "An unclean spirit is among us." As hard as it was to accept, I knew he was referring to me. I was the one with a demon.

Some people try to play the dumb role and pretend they don't know they need deliverance. Although you may not be able to put your finger on it, when you are in bondage you know something is wrong. I knew I was the one with the unclean spirit, and the man told me to step in the middle where everyone was standing. Stepping forward was my way of acknowledging I had a problem. When I stepped into the middle of the room, fear gripped me. The young man began to call unclean spirits out of me. My body began to jerk, and I was thrown from one side of the room to the other. Even Hollywood could not have made a movie like this.

Like I always say, "If you have a devil problem, you need a Jesus answer." That night I was delivered from demons and filled with the Holy Ghost with the evidence of speaking in other tongues. A lot of people don't want to deal with deliverance because it gets ugly. But the Lord told me not to focus on the ugliness of the process but the beauty of the outcome as a soul is set free from the bondage of darkness. My greatest joy is to see the light that emanates from a person's face after the devil has really let them go. This may sound crazy, but immediately after my deliverance I started laying hands on folk, and they were falling out under the power of God. I would not recommend this as an everyday occurrence. This was really a sign and a supernatural move of God.

ON FIRE FOR GOD

When I returned to Germany, I was lit up like a firecracker. Everything in my life did a turn around, but more important than anything, I refused to allow the devil to torment me again. I had a revelation of who Satan was and that I had power over him.

God began to use me. I founded a prison ministry and barracks ministry in Germany, and many souls were saved. However, I was not received well by the local churches. The things I walked in seemed foreign to them, and my presence intimidated them. I did not know any better than to offer to others what the Holy Ghost gave me. I just believed and practiced what the Bible said.

After being physically removed from two churches, God gave me a church home. It was the largest charismatic church in Frankfurt. The pastor supported me in every way. I met many Christian friends, and we were like family. After six months, I was placed in charge of the teenagers and was allowed to preach to them every Sunday. I had the liberty to cast out devils and get the teens filled with the Spirit as God led me.

> LIKE I ALWAYS SAY, "IF YOU HAVE A DEVIL PROBLEM, YOU NEED A JESUS ANSWER." THAT NIGHT I WAS DELIVERED FROM DEMONS AND FILLED WITH THE HOLY GHOST WITH THE EVIDENCE OF SPEAKING IN OTHER TONGUES.

When I received military orders that sent me to a German community an hour away, I started attending the full gospel service at the military installation. The chaplain was a black, female major, and she walked in the power of the Holy Ghost, too. Again I was placed over the teen ministry and children's church. I was even made the supervisor of three volunteers.

A DEMON BUSTER ON THE LOOSE!

When I went back to the States on leave, I was invited to give my testimony at a women's meeting at a local church I enjoyed attending.

When I arrived early to pray with the intercessors, I was shocked to hear that the guest speaker did not show up. *I* was the guest speaker!

Fear gripped my soul. I was not a preacher and could hardly find the books of the Bible. And I had less than fifteen minutes to prepare!

Despite all the objections I felt in my heart, my lips could not say no. I asked a young lady to follow me outside, daring not to speak until we were in a place where no one else could hear our conversation. I walked her down the stairs, outside the building, and to the back of the parking lot. I looked her straight in the eyes and said, "They want me to be the speaker!" She looked at me with almost no emotion and responded, "Baby, everything's gonna be all right. Let's pray." We prayed, and I trusted *her* faith, because God had just blown my mind.

When they introduced me, I stood at the podium, read a scripture, and opened my mouth to address the women. As I started to speak, the people could not stop laughing. It was going great! This was easier than I thought, and I was enjoying myself until the Holy Spirit told me to lay hands on people.

If I were sitting in the congregation that day, I don't believe I would have answered my own altar call. I told the people God wanted me to lay hands on them and that I had never done it before. I also told them they did not have to come to the altar if they didn't want to. I was hoping no one would respond, so it would all be over.

One lady walked up, and when I laid my hands on her, she fell to the floor. I stopped and looked at my hand. I could not believe what had happened. I had seen this type of manifestation of the Spirit before, but now I knew it was real. The power of God had moved through me. It was on! The devil never wanted this day to come, because I had a revelation that God wanted to use me.

A shocking thing happened next. Evangelist Mona, a well-known pastor, came up and stood in front of me for prayer. What is wrong with this picture? This was one of the most powerful evangelists in the city, and she wanted me to pray for her. When my hand touched her head, she fell under God's power also.

That day I ministered to approximately 150 women. Demons manifested, people were filled with the Spirit, and most of all, God received the glory. Truly, no one could take the credit for what happened with those women. It was at this meeting that Evangelist Mona prophesied to me, "Out of your belly shall flow Spoken Word Ministry!" The ministry had been birthed in the spirit and was about to manifest in the natural.

A WHOLE NEW SEASON

The most important thing about this experience was that it convinced me I had a call from God on my life—a call that was requiring me to go to another level. I now understood with certainty that God can use anybody He wanted to use. With all the military training, education, and natural abilities with which God had blessed me, nothing could have prepared me to speak that day. I had to depend totally on Him and recognize it is the anointing that destroys the yokes that hold people in bondage. Like never before, I saw the truth of Luke 19:40 in action: "And he answered and said unto them, I tell you that, if these should hold their peace, the stones would immediately cry out" (KJV).

When the others didn't make themselves available, God used me—a stone—though I was the least qualified to preach that day.

Many believers have become too comfortable sitting on the pew. There are prostitutes and drug dealers who may one day knock them off their seats to push them close to God. Those who have been saved from life on the streets are hungry for more of God.

People want Jesus! If evangelists will not win souls, prostitutes will. When pastors get weary in well doing, the drug dealers will feed God's sheep. The rocks will cry out!

The word for *stone* or *rock* in the Greek is *litho*. And it means "a stumbling stone, obstacle, or impediment." Someone who has a speech impediment does not have the natural ability to speak properly. A rock represents a lifeless, empty vessel. To sum it up, God is looking for those who do not have it all together, so He can use them for His glory.

> MANY BELIEVERS HAVE BECOME TOO COMFORTABLE SITTING ON THE PEW. THERE ARE PROSTITUTES AND DRUG DEALERS WHO MAY ONE DAY KNOCK THEM OFF THEIR SEATS TO PUSH THEM CLOSE TO GOD. THOSE WHO HAVE BEEN SAVED FROM LIFE ON THE STREETS ARE HUNGRY FOR MORE OF GOD.

When I returned to Frankfurt, I had transitioned to a new phase in my life. I had to get to know God and His power that was now flowing through me. I spent long hours with God for the next couple of years. He was consistently speaking to me. It was as if I was talking to my neighbor. I talked to Him early in the morning, during my lunch breaks, and late at night. I could not get enough of His presence.

God had blessed me with a Bible study in the barracks, which we called the Upper Room. I never intended to preach at the meetings, but I would recruit other preachers to hold services. I saw my role as gathering the crowd, which I was clearly gifted to do. Yet many times when I scheduled preachers to speak, they would call me the night before and say the Lord told them that *I* was the one who was supposed to be speaking.

The Lord had anointed me in such a way that people started to say I was a witch. This rumor did not come through heathens but through Christians. At that time, 95 percent of the people I ministered to had never known Christ. In contrast, those in the religious community "knew too much" to let a person like me pray for them. One day God spoke to me and said He was shutting down the Bible study in the barracks. I really struggled with giving it up, but I knew it was His ministry, not mine. God had many other faith-filled adventures in store for me.

CHAPTER 13

DESERT STORM

W AR WAS DECLARED in the Persian Gulf, and Operation
Desert Storm changed all of our lives. Fortunately, the
Lord moved me to a new duty position as the supply
sergeant for the 10th Armored Division Band. Two weeks after the
move, my old company was given orders to depart for Saudi Arabia. I was spared duty in Desert Storm, and it was a blessing for me
in more ways than one.

For years I had been in custody battles over my son. Mike-Mike's
father claimed that my military career would not allow me to provide an adequate lifestyle. After finally winning the custody battle,
I was about to be deployed to the battlefield in Saudi Arabia and
was required by law to sign my child over to the nearest relative.
Things looked very promising for Michael's father, but God had
promised me that I would be able to raise my child in the way he
should go.

Once the soldiers knew they were being deployed to war,
Hilda (my best friend) and I were the only ones who continued

to come to the Bible studies. Even though God had told me He was closing down the studies, I wanted to continue them until everyone left for the war. But people were trying to spend time with their families or just party and drink their fears away. They became subject to whatever the enemy could conjure up to keep them from worshiping God. But Hilda and I were faithful every Wednesday night. I would preach to her, and she would preach to me.

The Spirit of God had captured my life in such a way that even war couldn't take away my joy. The Lord had made promises to me before I found out my company was about to deploy. These promises did not line up with going to Saudi Arabia and signing my son over to his father. As I walked across the parking lot for my interview to be transferred to the 10th Armor Division Band, the Spirit of God spoke, "Go with this new position! Your present company is going somewhere, and you are not to go with them!"

That was it! I had my answer. God did not want me to deploy. His peace surrounded my mind, and I knew I was in His perfect will. No devil, war, or rank could override God's promise to me. After I transferred to the new division, it received deployment orders, too. Even so, I was convinced the Lord had promised He would keep me from being sent to war.

I shared what God had promised me with a few of my military friends, and word quickly spread around the post that I said my God would not let me go to war. I was the laughingstock of the compound. People I did not even know began to crack jokes about "my God" keeping me from going to war.

THE FAVOR OF THE LORD

God gave me favor during predeployment, and I was in charge of thousands of dollars of materials needed to equip the soldiers for battle. I was the supply sergeant, and it was my job to provide supplies, all the way from snacks to mosquito nets. During that time the Holy Spirit would give me revelations about procedures to help my commander prepare for wartime.

One day I passed by a soldier named Corporal Day, who was standing in the lobby crying. When I approached him, he explained that his wife had left him and wanted a divorce. I began to laugh and told him his problem wasn't big at all. I explained to him that his situation was small in God's eyes and that God could easily deal with his wife's heart. He accepted Jesus Christ as his Lord and Savior and was filled with the Holy Spirit with the evidence of speaking in other tongues. That night, his wife returned home and met with the corporal and me for prayer. He was knocked off his feet by the power of God.

Soon after Corporal Day's conversion, the commander made him my driver. This enabled us to spend many hours together praying in tongues. One day as the corporal and I were driving to a small town in Germany to pick up supplies, he confronted me about something that was bothering him. He asked me why everyone was saying I thought my God would keep me from going to war. I smiled at him and explained that the rumor was true: "God did tell me I was not going to war."

Corporal Day then asked if I would pray that God would keep him from going to war also. For some reason I said yes. I explained to him that God honors childlike faith and that if we agreed together with the right motives, He would answer our prayer.

One week later, a letter was published throughout the company with a list of personnel who would not deploy. Included on that list were my name, the corporal's name, and the name of an administrative clerk. Out of ten thousand soldiers, we were the only ones on the list who were not accepted due to pregnancy or a disability. God supernaturally kept me back!

HILDA'S MIRACLE

Hilda called me one night with excitement in her voice. She said God had spoken to her and that she would not deploy to Saudi Arabia. Before war was declared, she had orders for West Point Academy, and she felt the enemy was trying to rob her.

It was snowing that night, and I asked her to bring certain documents to my home so I could prepare an appeal for her deployment. I had never done this type of document before, but I knew I could do it if it was God's will for her to go to West Point.

On the way to my home, Hilda was involved in a car accident and called me from the emergency room. The Holy Spirit quickened my spirit, and I knew the devil was trying to block God's plan. When the devil lifts his head, he often ends up confirming God's will.

Now I knew I was on the right track, and I pursued the completion of the documents with fervency.

When we submitted the documents, however, they were rejected immediately. The army not only rejected our request but also recommended Hilda be released from the military early. I knew this was a form of retaliation, but my faith went to another level, because I knew the will of God in this situation. The case was not closed, as I would soon discover.

Despite many trials, my time overseas was the most awesome time I've experienced with God. I spent hours upon hours communing with the Lord, going to realms in God where few others dared go. My lunch breaks were spent evangelizing soldiers. I would pray about which table to sit at and claim the soul of the person sitting with me. I would often take soldiers to my room in the barracks where I would cast out devils and pray for them to be filled with the Holy Spirit.

One day I was not paying attention to where I would sit for lunch. I plopped down at a table and looked up to see a colonel sitting across from me. I was frustrated, because I knew he wasn't ready to be witnessed to. I did not want to offend him by moving, so I sat there and ate my lunch. I had been leading at least three to four people to the Lord daily and was irritated that my time was wasted sitting with someone who had no interest in the gospel. But God had another plan!

The Word of the Lord says our ways are not His ways and our thoughts are not His thoughts (Isa. 55:9). I introduced myself to the colonel and remained cordial. As I was speaking to him, his brass rank pin seemed to shine like gold. I noticed the name on his nametag, and it seemed oddly familiar.

Then I remembered who he was. My heart started racing. This could not be him. I was sitting at the table with the commanding officer who rejected Hilda's appeal! I was lit up with the anointing and could sense the favor of God on me. After I explained Hilda's entire situation, the colonel reviewed her papers again and sent them back to her—approved!

What an awesome God we serve! To my knowledge, Hilda was the only one who changed duty stations during deployment to war. It was absolutely unheard of, but all things are possible through Christ Jesus.

CHANGE OF PLANS

By the time the troops were loading equipment for deployment, Corporal Day was slacking in his walk with the Lord. It seemed that once he received what he wanted from God, he was content to lay back in apathy. I warned him that he had to continue to pray in the Spirit and give God the glory in his life. He responded with indifference, nodded his head, and carried on with a complacent attitude.

Two weeks before deployment, I was ordered to appear before the company commander. He was a Mormon, and he knew I was radically sold out to Jesus. Yet God would use him to provide all I needed to minister to the soldiers. We had an auditorium in our company that seated five hundred people. He would allow me to use the auditorium to have Christian conferences without ever complaining that I was using government property for religious purposes.

As I approached the commander's office, Corporal Day was passing by, cursing God. He looked me in the face and said he knew the Christian life was all a lie. He had orders to Saudi Arabia. He yelled that my orders were next to his—he would see me in Saudi. I stood before the commander, not knowing what to say or do. He briefed me that I had orders to Saudi and needed to sign the papers to send my son back to the U.S.

As I reached for the pen, the Holy Spirit said loudly, "Do not sign those papers!" But what did God expect me to do? Did I have to go to jail for disobeying a lawful order? I did the only thing I knew to do at the time, I asked the commander if I could be excused to go to the bathroom. On the way to the bathroom the voice of God told me to bind the devil. I prayed with fervency that day as Satan and I met face-to-face in the latrine.

I did not know how to bind demonic ranks, so my exact prayer was this: "Devil, I bind you, your mama, your daddy, and your entire generation. Loose me in Jesus' name!" This prayer may not make theological sense, but I didn't need it to make sense. I needed a miracle! God says He uses the foolish things to confound the wise.

The hordes of hell were coming up against my promise. Satan was using high-level rank in the natural realm, coupled with demonic infiltration, to take me out of God's perfect will. I didn't know much about spiritual warfare then; I just knew God.

I left my prayer closet in that latrine with another level of peace. Nothing else mattered, because I had done my part. I felt like Queen Esther: "If I die, I die!"

When I stood before the commander's desk the second time, he leaned over and whispered, "Don't tell anybody, but you are not going." Those words were music to my ears. It was not so much that I didn't want to be deployed; my praise report was that God fulfilled His promise!

As the other soldiers deployed, I was given a new job. I had the honor of escorting VIPs to the air base to wave good-bye to troops as their planes departed. All my peers who had made jokes about "my God" watched from the plane as I waved them off with a Holy Ghost smile. I did not rub it in, but I made sure the devils never forgot the victory I had won over them.

I know many soldiers sincerely prayed to be spared from deployment, and I asked God why He chose to keep Hilda and me back and not the others. The Lord reminded me of the time we went to the Bible study alone, despite circumstances. The Holy Spirit also spoke to my heart with a soft, gentle voice and said, "You were the only ones who believed I would do it."

THE HORDES OF HELL WERE COMING UP AGAINST MY PROMISE. SATAN WAS USING HIGH-LEVEL RANK IN THE NATURAL REALM, COUPLED WITH DEMONIC INFILTRATION, TO TAKE ME OUT OF GOD'S PERFECT WILL. I DIDN'T KNOW MUCH ABOUT SPIRITUAL WARFARE THEN; I JUST KNEW GOD.

CHAPTER 14

A Demon Buster Is Born

After the soldiers deployed to Saudi Arabia, all the soldiers left behind formed a rear detachment. I was one of the highest-ranking females in the group. My friend Hilda had one rank above mine, but she deployed to New York. The rear detachment consisted mostly of pregnant or injured soldiers.

One day I received an emergency call from a female staff sergeant who requested I come to the military hospital and pray for her baby. I was very surprised, because this female sergeant had often criticized me and called me a religious fanatic. When I entered the hospital room, the first sergeant of the rear detachment and several soldiers were present. The first sergeant was also an ordained deacon in one of the churches that had asked me not to attend their services anymore.

When I entered the room with another soldier, silence filled the room. The sergeant was pale, and she was leaning over a very sick baby with tubes in its head. She had not eaten for three days, because she feared her baby would die if she left the room. Several babies had died in the detachment that week.

The sergeant stood up and repented for all she had said about me. She said she didn't understand a lot about spiritual things, but she knew God answered my prayers. She wanted me to pray for her baby, and she personally wanted whatever I had in the Lord.

The other soldiers in the room did not think too well of her words, but I began to give God the glory. I took authority in that room and boldly suggested that we join hands in prayer. The first sergeant and soldiers hesitantly joined us in prayer. As I prayed in the Spirit, the female sergeant fell to the floor. I thought she had fallen under the power of God, but that was not the case.

When I reached down to pray for her, she looked up at me. Her face cracked, and her eyes rolled back into her head. A gruff voice came out of her, shouting and mocking, "Hallelujah! Thank You, Jesus!"

This scene was so frightening that the first sergeant and the other soldiers ran out the door. Every one of them professed to be a Christian, but a couple of them could not get out fast enough. Instead, they stood trembling with their backs against the wall. For some reason, I wasn't afraid. I've always been afraid of scary movies, but I wasn't afraid of her.

As I looked down at the sergeant's demon-possessed expressions, I heard the voice of God proclaim, "In My name they shall cast out devils!" I had never dealt with anything like this. At my church in Florida, we just commanded the devil to leave by faith. I did not realize he could take over a person in such a way.

As I commanded the demons to loose the woman, her body began to respond. By this time, the nurses' station was alerted that there was a problem in the room. The focus was no longer on the baby; now the mom was in trouble.

The Holy Spirit quickened my spirit and told me the hospital staff would admit her to the psychiatric ward for a nervous breakdown.

God said, "Do not let them!" I realized that the woman was unconscious and that devils were using her body. I walked her down several eral floors and out to the parking lot. As I walked her toward my car, her head was rolling around on her body like a paraplegic. She was growling and incoherent.

I had never seen a demonic manifestation like this before. I wanted to take her home and practice casting out devils. As I took her to my car, I would periodically whisper in her ear, "Wait until I get you to my house, devil."

After I managed to get her to my car, I was startled by a loud voice that said, "Halt!" Two male soldiers

> FOR SOME REASON, I WASN'T AFRAID. I'VE ALWAYS BEEN AFRAID OF SCARY MOVIES, BUT I WASN'T AFRAID OF HER. AS I LOOKED DOWN AT THE SERGEANT'S DEMON-POSSESSED EXPRESSIONS, I HEARD THE VOICE OF GOD PROCLAIM, "IN MY NAME THEY SHALL CAST OUT DEVILS!"

who were much bigger than me and who had more rank took her from my car and back into the emergency room. Under the circumstances, I felt as though my mission was over, but the soldier who accompanied me that day had a vision from God. She said God had told her we were not finished ministering to the sergeant and that we could not leave the hospital.

I believed Private James had heard from God, but my rank was on the line. I needed another witness. Before I could get the thought out of my mind, a nurse came out of the sergeant's room and asked us to guard her. We were dressed in duty uniform, and it was the ideal situation.

Private James and I laughed aloud, for we knew the devil had been defeated again. I walked in the room and jokingly said, "We're back!" The demons in this sergeant began to cry out. Her legs began to move as if she were running. She sat up like a stiff board and became silent. As I looked into her eyes, a horrible voice slowly released the words, "I know you!" I looked at Private James and said, "Isn't that a scripture from the Bible?" Even though I was a spiritual novice, the demons recognized who I was in Christ. God delivered the young sergeant that day, and I received new vision and revelation to set the captives free—for real!

BACKLASH

This incident took place on Friday, and on Monday morning, I was summoned to the rear detachment first sergeant's office. He was one of the people who ran out of the room when the demon manifested in the sergeant. He was my immediate supervisor and had been my number one critic on post.

The first sergeant commanded me to get at attention and began to read me my rights for court-martial procedure. I was put on barracks arrest and told to stand by as I was being considered for an Article XV charge. This meant I faced reduction in rank, a dishonorable discharge, and even military prison. I did not know what I had done. I was ordered not to pray in tongues, not to touch and agree with anyone in prayer, and not to lay hands on anyone.

The first sergeant was trying to charge me for the incident at the hospital. He literally called me a witch and told me to stand by for further counsel. He was clearly violating my rights as a soldier and as a believer. A spirit of religious stupor was using him, and he did not even realize it. As I sat outside his door, he called clerk after clerk with manual after manual to find an official charge. I prayed fervent prayers, loosing confusion to the enemy's camp.

When I finally stood before the first sergeant for him to read my charges, he stated that I was being charged with the following:

- The anointing with oil
- The laying on of hands
- Praying in tongues

As I heard the charges, a big smile broke out on my face as I almost burst into laughter. God had loosed confusion in the enemy's camp just as I had prayed! I don't think the first sergeant realized how silly his charges sounded. I informed him that he was coming up against my religious rights, and if he could not come up with better charges than that, I would counteract with a complaint for harassment. Despite this, the charges went through the legal channels, only to be thrown out in the end.

To Saudi After All

The Persian Gulf War was getting serious. We were on curfew, and Mike had to stay with one of our church members. One week before the fighting started, God spoke to my heart to go to Saudi Arabia. Isn't that just like God, to cancel my orders and then ask me to go with no orders?

I had to obey God at any cost, but how do you deploy to the battlefront with no orders? There were several reasons God wanted me in Saudi Arabia, but it was mainly to transport biblical materials.

Smuggling Bible materials into a Muslim country is not a very safe thing to do, but I had a vision from God. If God could give me orders to go, He would keep me safe. I decided to share my vision with Kenneth Hagin Ministries. Dr. Hagin had never heard of me, but I told him God had led me to contact him. He sent several thousand tracts and Bible study materials. With the help of the ministry and the army chaplain department, I was equipped to evangelize, but I still needed orders to deploy to the Middle East.

I finally had no option except to type my own orders. After much research, I had enough information to validate my travel to Saudi

Arabia as a courier. There were three senior officers who had to approve the documents, and none of them read the details. They all seemed distracted as I stood before them with my request for orders. I had two days to pack and get to the airport. I was going to the front lines.

All my Christian friends begged me not to go. They said if God wanted me to go, He would have sent me with everyone else. We were told horrible stories about living conditions over there. No one could believe I was foolish enough to volunteer. They didn't understand that I *had* to go—I had Holy Ghost orders!

I arrived in Saudi Arabia January 12, and I praised God for His faithfulness. The war was expected to officially start January 15. I distributed ministry materials throughout the compounds and witnessed to anyone I saw. I slept in the daytime and stayed up all night, leading people to the Lord.

DANNY AND KIM TOGETHER FOREVER!

After Desert Storm, I moved back to Florida and started my own ministry. Times were really hard in the first years. I never would have believed who God would use as the missing link for my ministry. When I got connected with Danny again, it was as if the dry bones of my ministry started to come together.

How could two people, who had grown so far apart, all of a sudden drift back together? At the time I felt that I was free to do the ministry God had called me to do. I found out, though, God had other plans, but I was not so anxious to jump on the boat.

I did not believe that Danny could serve God like me! I knew he was involved in Freemasonry, a fraternal order, and he did drugs. I was also not enthused about sharing him with three or four other ladies. I was fasting and praying with an elderly lady in Fort Lauderdale, Florida. We had been praying for days when the Lord spoke to me and said, "I am going to save Danny!"

I literally said to God, "God, You know he cannot be saved!"

The quiet response I received from God made me jump into intercession for Danny's soul. God was not playing! Then God said to me, "Now call him!" I fussed with Him about not having a contact number for Danny, and He supernaturally revealed to me how to get in contact with Danny.

I called him on a pager, and he immediately called me back. I could not believe it! I told him that I was in Fort Lauderdale and that I was about to preach. He said, "What a coincidence. I am on my way to Fort Lauderdale to pick up a package." When Danny said he would come by the church to see me, my heart started beating fast, but it wasn't a "love jones."

I thought to myself, *Package? What kind of package?* I hadn't been involved in illegal activities in years. I started binding the devil, calling him a liar and declaring that I was not going back to Satan!

I was in the mirror talking to myself about how Danny did not know the God I served, and if he tried anything slick, he would not stand a chance. I preached in a little church no bigger than a shack that night, but it was a Holy Ghost–filled shack. The building was jumping!

When Danny arrived, I was preaching, and the church had a speaker on the outside of the building. Danny was sitting in the car, listening to my sermon. At the time, I had a guy traveling with me from uptown named "Butterball." I called Butterball to the pulpit to give his testimony.

Butterball, a nine-time convicted felon, testified using some not so church-friendly words. He ended by saying, "I would like to thank Pastor Kim for inviting me to the 'bull-pit' to give my testimony; I am her 'almond-bearer.'" Surely he was unchurched, but his heart was in the right place.

The religious people were shocked, but Danny jumped out of his car to see who Butterball was. Danny had never been in church before except to deliver drugs to crooked preachers. By the time Danny entered the door, people were getting devils cast out of them and speaking in tongues. Danny sat in the back of the church with his mouth open.

He later shared with me that his first thought of me was that I was beating the people out of their money and putting on a show. But when he saw little babies falling under the power of God, he knew it was real. Danny took me home that night, and we sat in the parking lot until 5:00 a.m. as he asked me questions about Jesus.

Butterball was peeping out of one window, and the mother I was traveling with was peering out of the other window. Danny had a woman and drugs waiting on him in a hotel room, but I led Danny to the Lord that night.

To tell the truth, after he repeated the sinner's prayer, I thought his conversion was just a temporary thing, but Danny begged me to teach him about Jesus. I didn't take him serious at the time, but God took him serious. Danny never picked up his package that weekend, and he has been faithfully serving Jesus since that night. His deliverance is another story.

DANNY GETS DELIVERED

Danny would send large financial contributions to my church. He even sent a crew to fix the old building one time. He would meet me on the road and help me sell my material. Still, I didn't see him as my man. I was so excited about his zeal for the Lord, but he still had to be delivered from so many things.

He still had a lot of women, smoked marijuana, snorted cocaine, and smoked cigarettes. One night he came to a church meeting and later knocked on my hotel door. He confessed that every time he was around me, his stomach felt funny. I peeped in the room and told my roommate, a young lady in my ministry, that he was ready for deliverance.

Danny later told us that he had cocaine in one pocket and marijuana in the other. When we laid hands on him he said he thought, *I am in this room with two fine women; the party is on!* No matter how much he sought God, the lust demons in him had control. I placed my mouth close to his ear and said, "Come out, you lust demon, in the name of Jesus!"

It scared Danny so bad, because he thought I had read his mind. He fell on the floor gagging and throwing up demons. His neck blew up as big as a bowling ball when we called out the male chauvinist spirit of pride. We worked Casanova over for a while!

From that time forward, Danny never smoked another cigarette. He threw away his dope, rode away, and could not stop praying in tongues. After a period of time, God told me Danny was, and always had been, my husband. When he asked me to marry him, I could not believe my ears. God gave me the desire of my heart even when my mind could not discern it.

Chapter 15

Ordained and Activated

OVER THE YEARS, God has always dealt with me concerning giving. One night I sensed His Spirit pulling me aside. He told me there would be no more "month-to-month faith." Not only did God want me to believe I could be debt free, but He also wanted me to increase my giving at a whole new level.

I had seldom watched Pastor Rod Parsley on television, but God prompted me to plant a seed in his ministry. He also instructed me to do something I had never done before—get two prayer cloths and put one cloth under my mattress and the other under my pulpit. I obeyed, and our congregation quickly grew to one hundred members in only a few months. From that time until now, our ministry's financial status has been just as God said— abundant provision.

The Lord also told me to purchase a very expensive thirty-foot recreation vehicle (RV)—$60,000 to be exact. Just about everyone I knew criticized me for purchasing a RV. God told me to call it Demon-Buster Mobile and to use it for evangelism.

No one seemed to be able to catch the vision, but God spoke to me. We were a few thousand dollars from purchasing the vehicle when God told me to plant another seed in Pastor Parsley's ministry. This time I was directed to personally deliver it.

God's instruction was clear on this, but the provision was a little foggy. The Lord also said that Pastor Parsley would ordain me. How could this be? I did not know where to start, but we attended the World Harvest Pastors' Conference.

As we walked in the door, we watched Pastor Parsley on a screen. He had asked all pastors who were to be ordained to come forward. I looked at my husband and said, "That's us!" We immediately went into the sanctuary and stood at the front of the altar with all the other pastors. What a chance I took!

As Pastor Parsley came down the prayer line, he laid hands on us, and we fell under the power of God. I knew we were in the Lord's perfect will. As the word of the Lord was going forth in power, the Holy Spirit quietly spoke to me and said, "Go to the bonfire area." When we arrived, a well-dressed man greeted us. We told him Pastor Parsley had ordained us.

The man was puzzled, because he was the director of that department and didn't recognize my name. I smiled and let him know

> RELIGION WOULD SAY I WAS OUT OF ORDER, BUT THOSE WHO HAVE A RELATIONSHIP WITH GOD UNDERSTAND THAT HE WILL TAKE A FOOLISH THING AND CONFOUND THE WISE. A MONTH LATER I WAS OFFICIALLY ACCEPTED INTO THE MINISTERIAL ALLIANCE, BUT I KNEW AN IMPARTATION HAD ALREADY TAKEN PLACE.

that God told me to walk down that aisle and that it would work out for everyone's good. The man gave me a membership packet for us to complete to be members of the fellowship.

Religion would say I was out of order, but those who have a relationship with God understand that He will take a foolish thing and confound the wise. I knew an impartation had already taken place.

Mr. Yoder, the well-dressed man at the bonfire, now jokes with me about my ordination service with Pastor Parsley. Today, my husband and I are armorbearers who undergird Pastor Parsley financially and in prayer.

Within five months after Pastor Parsley laid hands on my husband and me, spiritual doors opened that released Spoken Word Ministries to the nations. I once had dinner with Pastor Parsley and shared our testimony with him about the supernatural ordination and impartation that we received at the pastors' conference.

Pastor Parsley laughed as he leaned back in his chair and thought it was quite a testimony. He even sent a camera crew to our church and to our home to record our testimony. If God leads you into a situation, He covers all the bases.

THE DEMON BUSTER

God supernaturally allowed us to drive that brand-new vehicle off the lot. I would not let anyone see it until I had put the words *Demon-Buster Mobile* on it. We used the vehicle for street evangelism, and it really caught the attention of people. The first time we put it on the road was to visit a deliverance minister named Bob Larson.

The Demon-Buster Mobile was so big we couldn't find a place to park, so I proudly parked it in front of the church. Devil worshipers filled the church that day. Even today they follow after Bob dressed in black "witchcraft drag" and painted faces. They even have voodoo dolls and posters of Bob Larson.

I had never been so excited in my life. The meeting went well, and I even interviewed a few devil worshipers. We were waiting outside in the Demon-Buster Mobile, and a long train of cars with a police escort pulled up on the side of us. Two men stepped out of the vehicle and knocked on the door of the RV. It was Bob Larson and one of Billy Graham's associates.

> WITH BISHOPS LINED ACROSS THE FRONT STAGE, NEEDLESS TO SAY, I WAS NOT ANXIOUS TO RUN AROUND A CROWD OF THREE THOUSAND PEOPLE. YET GOD CONTINUED TO BID ME TO RUN. FINALLY, THE SPIRIT SAID, "IF YOU RUN, I WILL TEAR DOWN STRONGHOLDS!"

My heart was beating so fast I could hardly catch my breath. Mr. Larson said he only wanted to know who was crazy enough to have a vehicle like that. Before leaving with his entourage, he invited me to be on his radio broadcast. I thought it was very nice of him to have me on his radio broadcast, and I thanked God for the opportunity.

NEW DOORS OPENING

The year 1998 was almost gone, and God spoke to me about great things in my future ministry as He always does. The word of the Lord came to me in December: "At the beginning of the year to come, I shall put you in the company of those who are considered giants in the ministry, and they shall be drawn by the genuineness of your faith."

Like every other year, I received the word of the Lord and pressed toward it. I did not realize that this time God's "beginning of the year" lined up with mine.

By the middle of January, I received a letter from Mission America about a group of ministers who were meeting to discuss deliverance issues in the nation. The names on the list were those I had only seen on television and in bookstores. I knew I had to make this trip. It was not until a week later that I realized my name was listed as a pastor with this group. Concerned that they had made a mistake, I called to see if they had the right Kim Daniels. Indeed, I was the right one.

I later found out that Bob Larson had recommended me as "the lady with the Demon-Buster Mobile." God truly takes the foolish things to confound the wise. At that meeting, I met Dr. C. Peter Wagner, Chuck Pierce, and many other great men and women of God in the Spiritual Warfare Network. In the meeting, we were asked to seek God concerning what He was saying about deliverance in America. This is the message that God gave to me to tell them: warfare and deliverance require a high level of discipline and obedience to God. That same message is a word for you, too.

LEARNING OBEDIENCE

Not long after my ordination, I attended a major Church of God conference. The auditorium was packed, and bishops from around the country were present. I was enjoying the preaching, and the music in the background enhanced the moment. The Spirit of God came on me in a special way; it seemed as if the Holy Spirit was tickling me. While sitting in my chair, I fell under the power of God three or four times.

When I stood up, a tickling sensation shot throughout my body. The thing that made this occurrence so strange is that no one else was responding this way. Then the word of the Lord came to me, "Run around the building!"

With bishops lined across the front stage, needless to say, I was not anxious to run around a crowd of three thousand people. Yet

God continued to bid me to run. Finally, the Spirit said, "If you run, I will tear down strongholds!"

Based on those words, I ran as fast as I could. I had a long, flowing dress on, so I gathered it to my knees and ran like a wild woman. My bishop said that I ran by the podium so fast he couldn't tell who I was.

When I finished running, I fell under the power of the Spirit, and God began to speak to me. He said by this time next year, the people would say, "This is why she was running." The Church of God meeting was held in June 1998, and in July 1999, I was speaking at the National Congress on Deliverance hosted by Dr. C. Peter Wagner.

CHAPTER 16

A NEW SEASON

W ELL, I MADE it! I made it to Colorado Springs, despite
all the obstacles. I was a guest speaker at the National
Congress on Deliverance Conference, and my mind
couldn't catch up with my body. The host of the event was one
of the most respected leaders in spiritual warfare and deliverance
ministry: Dr. C. Peter Wagner.

As I eased my way past many of the conference-goers, I thought
to myself, *This is a dream!* I could sense expectancy in the air, and I
knew a new beginning was about to take place in my life.

Every time I thought about speaking to such a large crowd, my
heart would beat fast. I had never preached to more than five hundred people, plus I was the only speaker there who was not nation-
ally or internationally known. My original assignment was to do a
workshop in the main arena and a breakout session after another
speaker cancelled, but God had another plan!

I met a prophet named David Guy during the first day of the
conference. He looked at me at said, "Sister, God is about to drop

the bomb!" I did not know what he meant, but when I looked into his eyes I believed what he said.

There was another apostle named John Eckhardt speaking at the meeting. Though I did not know him, I had heard of him. Prophet Guy told me that Apostle Eckhardt would be my spiritual father. I thought to myself, *No!* Apostle Eckhardt seemed to be a very serious, reserved type of man, and I couldn't imagine myself hanging out with him.

Prophet Guy got down on his knees with me, and we began to pray about the things God had shown him. God confirmed to me in a matter of moments that He was hooking me up with John Eckhardt from Crusaders Ministries in Chicago. Afterward, I was ready to do the will of the Lord.

One hour before I ministered, I went to Chuck Pierce, who was the assistant to Dr. Wagner. I told him that God had given me two songs to rap before I preached. This was unheard of because Peter Wagner's conferences ran in an orderly fashion—no last minute unnecessary changes. When I told Chuck what I had in mind, it didn't make matters any better.

"Yes," I told him, "God wants me to rap!" Chuck Pierce looked at me with the most serious look I had ever seen and said, "I will not ask Peter Wagner if you can rap!" I don't believe Chuck had a problem with rap music; it's just that it had never been done before. There it was again—another mold was about to be broken. This time it was not planned by me; God was breaking the mold.

Eventually, Chuck got the message to Dr. Wagner, and he gave me approval to rap one song. As the street beat filled the sanctuary, I began to sing, "We gonna cast the devil out!" The crowd went crazy! Who was in the crowd? Mostly middle- to upper-class white Christians and people from around the world.

Before I could finish rapping, the crowds bombarded my product tables, and I practically sold out of music and other resources. Peter Wagner nudged my husband, "Tell her to sing another song." When I sang the lyrics, "Tear the roof of the sucker," "Who dat trying to be bad?," and "Hey ho, devil, you gotta go!," the atmosphere shifted and a new climate was set.

During my first session with over three thousand believers, I warned them that my breakout session was only for those who were serious about deliverance. I was scheduled to speak in a gymnasium that seated about seven hundred, and two other speakers were to speak in arenas that seated fifteen hundred and three thousand. I started my breakout session with wall-to-wall people in that gymnasium.

While I was ministering, I could hear the crowd outside my room chanting, "We want Kim!" I could not believe my ears! The crowd was lined up in the hall, because the gymnasium was full to capacity. People were literally sitting at my feet during the session.

I had mixed emotions. I was excited, because I could not believe what God was doing in my ministry, but I was also embarrassed that they were chanting my name. I ignored the noise and continued to try and deliver my message when Peter Wagner and Chuck Pierce walked in the door. Peter yelled, "Stop the service!" *What did he mean stop the service?* I thought to myself. *I am in the middle of my message.*

EVENTUALLY, CHUCK GOT THE MESSAGE TO DR. WAGNER, AND HE GAVE ME APPROVAL TO RAP ONE SONG. AS THE STREET BEAT FILLED THE SANCTUARY I BEGAN TO SING, "WE GONNA CAST THE DEVIL OUT!" THE CROWD WENT CRAZY! WHO WAS IN THE CROWD? MOSTLY MIDDLE- TO UPPER-CLASS WHITE CHRISTIANS AND PEOPLE FROM AROUND THE WORLD.

You don't just stop a preacher in the middle of a scripture, but we did that day! Peter kindly asked the crowd to go to other sessions to hear the other speakers. Then he said the words that I will never forget: "Kim Daniels will be the keynote speaker tonight at the seven o'clock service."

Chuck Pierce so humbly and graciously agreed to allow Peter to move me into his time slot. As I was walking down the halls, people were trying to touch me, wanting to meet the "Demon Buster."

I passed through the crowd and veered off into a small room and sat there with my mouth open. I would occasionally peep out the door and pinch myself to prove that I wasn't dreaming. Little did I know, my team members who were called "the Dirty Dozen" had lines of people outside the prayer room who refused to leave until they received prayer. I can still say today that I have never seen a move of God like I saw in those prayer rooms at the Congress on Deliverance. For the previous six months, we too had to fast, pray, train, and get delivered so we could function as a unified team. As a result, God showed up and showed out! We literally saw homosexual men turn masculine again.

There were teams from around the world, and God used all of them mightily, but people were saying there was a special anointing on the Dirty Dozen that day. The Dirty Dozen was headed by my husband, Ardell, and consisted of twelve ex-drug addicts, prostitutes, homosexuals, and street dealers. Everyone from churchgoers to multimillionaires was miraculously set free by the power of God. We are still receiving testimonies from people who are experiencing the blessings of that meeting.

Though we had huge spiritual success at the conference, getting to the event was another story. I had to come up with airplane tickets for thirty people and resources for my product table. That was the first time I duplicated and packaged my own sermons and book to sell at a conference.

My husband and my children reproduced over six thousand tapes with a machine that duplicated cassettes one tape at a time.

We worked on the project day and night for two weeks. All we had was a family assembly line, but the material was packaged and delivered on time. It was a lot of hard work, but it was worth every minute. And if I had to do it again, I would. We also needed hotel rooms for people who couldn't afford to pay for a room. Thank God, He supernaturally provided everything!

Before the conference, the administrative staff of Wagner Institute called me to say I would do a book signing. I did not have the nerve to tell them that I didn't have a book, so months before the conference, I wrote a book and published it myself. The book had many errors, but we sold over five hundred copies to people from other nations.

As I stood on the stage at the service that night I declared, "God is releasing a fresh anointing in the earth realm!" When I uttered the last, the venue shook. Everyone in the building felt it and heard it. For minutes no one moved. I was the speaker, and I was scared half to death. A prophetic word went forth, and I continued preaching.

Traditionally, the church has reached out to save people in the

THE DIRTY DOZEN WAS HEADED BY MY HUSBAND, ARDELL, AND CONSISTED OF TWELVE EX-DRUG ADDICTS, PROSTITUTES, HOMOSEXUALS, AND STREET DEALERS. EVERYONE FROM CHURCHGOERS TO MULTIMILLIONAIRES WAS MIRACULOUSLY SET FREE BY THE POWER OF GOD. WE ARE STILL RECEIVING TESTIMONIES FROM PEOPLE WHO ARE EXPERIENCING THE BLESSINGS OF THAT MEETING.

inner city. This time God loosed a boomerang anointing and turned it around. The inner city came to save the church! When I returned from Colorado Springs, my phones were ringing off the hook. God had shifted my ministry to international status overnight. My calendar went from empty to full—eighteen months out—with national and international engagements.

I received calls from forty states in two days, and three millionaires flew in and were waiting to talk with me when I arrived back in my city. Doors started to open for my ministry July 1999, and it has not stopped yet. Over the last six years, my husband and I have traveled consistently around the world, including every state in this nation. It was clear. The church wanted something that was real and people who were genuine. Since I've told you about my new season, which I call "The Season of the Last," I think it's important you know what that really means. Check it out!

THE SEASON OF THE LAST

I was excited to see that the most valuable player of the NFL Super Bowl in 2000 was Kurt Warner. He was a stock boy in a grocery store before God broke him out into his destiny. Kurt's story is a reminder to me that we are living in the "season of the last." This is spoken of in the Gospels of Matthew and Mark, where Jesus says the last shall be first and the first shall be last. (See Matthew 19:30 and Mark 10:31.)

The Greek translation of the word *last* is *eschatos*, and it means "uttermost." Uttermost means "to the greatest degree possible." So not only does the word mean "last," but it means last to the lowest degree possible. This is an encouraging word to people the enemy has oppressed or held in demonic depths.

If you have been pushed to your lowest point in life, I prophesy a catapulting anointing come upon you! You will receive this anointing as restitution for your oppression. The Bible declares the more the children of Israel were oppressed, the more they multiplied. It is "due season" for those who have been last, but only if they will allow God to hold them back. For example, a slingshot only works effectively if the band is stretched back far enough. The more the band is pulled, the greater the release! Many people disqualify others who are considered "the last." But I know a God who takes what another man considers trash and makes treasure of it.

There is a popular television show called *Pimp My Ride*. The slang word *pimp* means to "make like new." On the show, they transform old, raggedy cars into brand-new cars. When a car is pimped, it has to be torn apart first. Then they put televisions and state-of-the-art sound systems in these jalopies. They also reupholster the insides of the cars and make them look perfectly new.

> IF YOU HAVE BEEN PUSHED TO YOUR LOWEST POINT IN LIFE, I PROPHESY A CATAPULTING ANOINTING COME UPON YOU! YOU WILL RECEIVE THIS ANOINTING AS RESTITUTION FOR YOUR OPPRESSION. THE BIBLE DECLARES THE MORE THE CHILDREN OF ISRAEL WERE OPPRESSED, THE MORE THEY MULTIPLIED. IT IS "DUE SEASON" FOR THOSE WHO HAVE BEEN LAST, BUT ONLY IF THEY WILL ALLOW GOD TO HOLD THEM BACK.

Isn't this exactly what God does to us? He upgrades our seeing and hearing and changes us totally on the inside. Old things pass away, and everything becomes new! So when you see a person who was once broken down made better than before, recognize that they have "officially" been pimped!

Many cannot receive a spiritual "upgrade" from God because they are not willing to endure the "tearing down." But the reward for those who will allow God to strip them inwardly is that they will one day become "the first." Are you bold enough to ask God to "pimp" your life?

CHAPTER 17

IN THE OCCULT

MANY DOORS HAVE opened for the deliverance team of Spoken Word Ministries. In 2000, we traveled to New Orleans to a spiritual warfare conference. As we boarded the airplane, I smelled the stench of witchcraft spirits at the entrance of the door. I quickly alerted my team that something was going on in the spirit, and I asked them to pray in tongues under their breath.

When I reached my seat, I noticed sitting across from me two rows up was a very strange-looking man. His face was jet black with burn-mark stripes across his cheeks like some tribal people do in Africa. In the back of his head were knots that looked like large marbles. When he turned around, I saw that his eyes were fire red. I don't believe you had to be sharp in discernment to know that he was from the other side.

I could feel electricity in the air, and it was not of God. An eerie heaviness tried to take over the atmosphere, and I was sure this man was a voodoo priest. All of a sudden it came to me that we were traveling to New Orleans to minister at this warfare conference during Mardi Gras. This was great timing to learn warfare, but if I had known earlier what was happening in the city, I would have chosen another week!

At the beginning of my ministry, God gave me the gift of discernment, meaning I can discern good and evil spirits. As I mature in God, He continually sharpens my gift. I have learned to identify spirits by smell, appearance, and assignment, and I can especially discern the voice of God. Just as a bank teller is trained to detect counterfeit money, I can recognize human beings who have surrendered their lives to the devil.

When I laid eyes on this voodoo doctor, I knew he meant business. He wasn't there to pass licks in the spirit.

People have affectionately called us Demon Busters because they have witnessed the anointing that operates on our lives through warfare and deliverance. This was a day we had to either bust or be busted! There were new team members traveling with us, and I was concerned about them becoming fearful. So I did what I do best—broke the mold! We began singing warfare rap songs—out loud—on the plane.

We prayed in tongues, we praised God, and we acted just like we weren't supposed to act on that plane. We blew the devil's mind. Can you imagine a high-level witch doctor sitting next to a group of believers from the inner city rapping "Oops Upside Your Head," "Who Dat Trying to Be Bad?," and "Hey, Ho, Devil, You Gotta Go"?

We tormented the demons in him to the point where he jumped up from his seat and ran to the bathroom. The ironic thing is that he stayed in the bathroom for most of the flight. This just encouraged us even more and took our praise to another level. I must admit that I enjoyed every minute of it.

Once we arrived in New Orleans, we had a powerful meeting with the pastors who really had a burden to see the captives set free. We saw supernatural manifestations of God in that meeting.

While folk were worshiping the devil around the corner, we purposed in our hearts to glorify our God. After the service, the devil was waiting for us at the hotel. Demonic manifestations that I had never experienced before began to occur.

The first thing I noticed were the birds squawking in my hotel room wall. The person I was talking to on the phone could hear them also. I thought of a story I once read in one of Benson Idahosa's books.

Once during a meeting, voodoo doctors in his country sent giant birds to scare people away from the meeting. Benson commanded the birds to die, in the name of Jesus, and the birds dropped dead. I had nothing to lose, so I did the same thing. I praised God as the eerie sounds of the birds ceased when I commanded them to die in Jesus' name.

We finished ministering, but the pastor of the church called and asked if we could stay one more day. The Lord had given me stern instructions to minister and then immediately return home. The pastor was so nice. She asked me to please stay, because the people needed our ministry in New Orleans.

I learned a very important lesson at this meeting. I cannot help anyone if God is not with me. Because I disobeyed the Lord's instruction, the anointing had lifted, but we tried to keep going. In my heart I wanted to obey the Lord and go home, but I didn't know how to tell that precious pastor no. I agreed to stay another day; surely God would understand if I stayed to help more people get free.

The next morning around 4:00 a.m., the Lord awakened me with an urgency to pray. I was praying with my face toward the sofa. My husband was in the bedroom in our suite, and I was in the sitting room. Suddenly the stench of sulfur filled the room. I had never smelled sulfur in my life, yet I could discern the odor. Then the word *hell* came to my mind.

When I tried to turn my face from the sofa, I briefly saw what looked like the predator creature from the 1986 movie. Then something grabbed my face and covered my mouth, and I was not asleep! Whenever I have experienced a demonic attack, the devil is always trying to shut my mouth. I could only see the hand as it covered my mouth, but I could tell it was an ectoplasm—the materialization of an astral body or a spiritual entity. I could see through the hand as though it was a form of clear jelly.

I knew that I was in the spirit realm, and God had allowed me to see into the *other* kingdom. As the force grabbed me, I started quoting the scripture "Greater is He that is in me than he that is in the world"! (See 1 John 4:4.)

This was not the attack of a nightmare spirit. Remember, I wasn't asleep; I was praying! Nightmare spirits, often called "hanks" or a witch that rides a person, attack the physical body while the victim is asleep.

> CAN YOU IMAGINE A HIGH-LEVEL WITCH DOCTOR SITTING NEXT TO A GROUP OF BELIEVERS FROM THE INNER CITY RAPPING "OOPS UPSIDE YOUR HEAD," "WHO DAT TRYING TO BE BAD?," AND "HEY, HO, DEVIL, YOU GOTTA GO"? WE TORMENTED THE DEMONS IN HIM TO THE POINT WHERE HE JUMPED UP FROM HIS SEAT AND RAN TO THE BATHROOM.

The astral body (spirit of a person) is often conscious of the attack. Most people I have interviewed concerning this type of occurrence told me that when their spirit man began to call on Jesus, the unseen force released them.

Incubus and Succubus, which are mentioned in Webster's dictionary, are other prominent nightmare spirits that come to torture people. These two demonic beings attack people while they are asleep, releasing perversion and lust. Most of the time the victims will not discuss such an encounter, because the enemy either tricks them into believing it was only a dream or they are too embarrassed to discuss it.

Genesis 6:2 says that the sons of God came from heaven and had intercourse with the daughters of men. This is a reference of demons having sex with humans. It brings another light to the revelation of how evil the imaginations of men were before God wiped out the earth with the flood.

The Hebrew translation of the word *imagination* is *yatsar*. It means the way the human mind is molded, framed, or squeezed into shape. In other words, God knew that through evil imagination, which is witchcraft, the sinister works of man would wax worse.

Rebellion is as the sin of witchcraft, and whenever we attempt to pervert the order of God, wickedness reigns. I have probably lost a few folk with my creature-feature testimony, but please understand; the devil is real! If it weren't for the Holy Ghost holding back the hordes from the caverns and vortexes of hell, we wouldn't have to pay to see a horror show.

The Bible says the gates of hell shall not prevail against the church. The word *gates* in the Greek is *pule*, which means "portal" or "entrances." The verse describes the way demons travel through the vortexes of hell to the earthly realm. The "gates" of hell spoken of in Matthew 16:18 are the jaws of Hades that spew demons on the earth to be released for their satanic assignments.

The Bible declares that Satan and his imps will not prevail against the church, but it doesn't say they won't try. Weapons will form, but they will not prosper. (See Isaiah 54:17.)

REGAINING MY VOICE

One month after our ministry trip to New Orleans, I was having problems with my voice. In fact, it was getting worse. One night I received a call from a woman who had been a leader in thirty-six different cults. At the time I talked with her, she had been delivered for ten years. She would only discuss her prior life as a witch when the Holy Spirit prompted her. For the sake of confidentiality, I'll refer to her as Sister Free.

Sister Free told me that witches had pronounced viruses on my vocal cords. She went on to tell me how she had cursed the voices of many of God's people when she worked on the other side. Not only did she share the problem with me, but she also gave me the solution. She told me about some natural and spiritual steps I could take to counteract the enemy's attack.

> GOD REALLY DOES HAVE A SENSE OF HUMOR! ONE OF MY MAIN STRENGTHS AS A BELIEVER IS THAT I HAVE NO RESPECT FOR EVIL.

The woman said the witches had attacked my voice, because they wanted to silence the "voice of John the Baptist" in my life. She explained that witches claim this is why John the Baptist's head was cut off—to shut his mouth.

A few days later God gave me dreams and visions of sorcerers, voodoo doctors, and witches around the world who had sewn up the mouths of voodoo dolls. Praise God, I broke the curse that comes against "the voice that cries out in the wilderness." My voice was restored. It was better than ever. Satan's minion was sent back to him for torment because he could not complete his mission.

Remember the voodoo doctor on the airplane? Well, he came to me in a dream. He was on the plane telling me, "I am the man from the plane." His face appeared as a zombie. God had already told us to bind this spirit when we first encountered his presence. Sister Free said the voodoo doctor came to deliver a curse while

I was sleeping. As a former shaman, Sister Free explained that some curses cannot be sent, but must be delivered. This is one of the main jobs of shamans, people who conjure fetishes in order to assign demons to objects so the objects will carry the curses.

In the dream, the voodoo doctor took me to the airplane door, opened it, and showed me all that was his. As he reached out his hand to point toward what he was showing me, he said, "If you obey me, you could have all this."

When I looked down, there were beautiful islands, and all the buildings had large voodoo masks on the top of them. Before he offered me anything, I booted him off the airplane with my foot. Today, I have a symbol on my Web site with a foot continuously kicking the devil.

God really does have a sense of humor! One of my main strengths as a believer is that I have no respect for evil.

CHAPTER 18

GENERATIONAL BLESSINGS

I WILL NEVER FORGET when God saved me and took me off the track circuit while training for the Olympics. I was at the peak of my career. I had just started my first dose of anabolic steroids, and I was pumped for victory.

How could God ask me to stop running at the height of my career? He told me to walk away from it—all of it! But He promised that my seed would accomplish what I didn't.

I heard the Word of the Lord clearly that day and obeyed Him. I quit using steroids and separated myself from anything that would displease Him.

God promised me that His mercy would be extended to me for a thousand generations. The Hebrew word for *mercy*, pronounced *kheh-sed*, is found in Exodus 20:6. One meaning for this word is "favor." I thank God for a thousand generations of favor. My heart gets excited when I think about what is in store for future generations in my bloodline. The curse is broken, praise God!

My children have an inheritance that affords them the opportunity to fulfill their destiny in God. It is my prayer that my great-great-great-grandchildren will tell stories about my life: how I was not perfect, but that I served God with all my heart.

In my book *From a Mess to a Miracle*, I wrote about the troubles I had with my oldest son, Michael. He had problems with ungodly associations, drug abuse, and incarceration. His driver's license had been revoked, and he had other issues. Despite everything, I knew my son's problems were temporary. The Bible says that what we see is temporary, but what we cannot see is eternal. I chose to believe in what I couldn't see in Michael.

The Greek translation of the word *temporary* is *proskairos*. The word *kairos* means "timing of God." The prefix *pros* means "ahead of" or "before." *Proskairos* means "getting ahead of the timing of God."

The Bible says many people receive the Word of God with joy, but when persecution comes, they endure only for a time or temporarily. The word *time* in this context is *proskairos* in the Greek. When it comes to our children and what God has for them, we must direct our faith toward eternal things.

THE PROPHECY

When Michael was eight years old, it was prophesied that he would play professional football. Many obstacles came his way concerning the promise. Because I traveled a lot while in the military, Mike was unable to play football. When we finally came back to the United States, a spirit of rebellion took over my son's mind. The fruits of this rebellion were bad grades, constant struggles with authority, and brushes with the law.

But God put my son in a place where he had to make right choices or else. Deuteronomy 28 reveals to us the promises of blessings God has for His people if we obey Him. The passage also warns that these blessings are conditional.

Despite his grades, Grambling University committed to place

Michael in a special academic program to meet eligibility requirements. It wasn't long, though, before he transferred to Florida State
University on a track scholarship. This seemed like a dangerous
switch, because Mike had no experience in track and field.

In three years he became the second fastest quarter-mile runner
ever to attend the university. Though I ran relay on a championship
team, my name never made it in the record books. I thank God that
my son went where I could not go, just as the Lord had promised.

Mike tried to make the transition to football during his last year
of college, but he didn't make it. The crowd he was hanging around
during his short success amounted to one thing—trouble!

My son was involved in incident after incident. He was about to
become a convicted felon for the rest of his life. God reminded me
that, just like Mike, my troubles also started my third year in college at Florida State. This was no coincidence.

When I understood the connection between my life and my
son's problems, I took authority over my past in the name of Jesus.
I declared that the generational curse was broken! I drove up and
down Interstate 10 for five hours, from Jacksonville to Tallahassee,
Florida, binding the devil.

I was slinging oil and pleading, *The blood of Jesus!* I made up my
mind that the devil could not have my child. The state's attorney,
lawyers, and professionals involved swore that my son would do at
least three years as a convicted felon. Despite their predictions, the
hand of God intervened. It was divine destiny!

My son had a date with destiny, and though the enemy tried to
delay him, God caused supernatural synchronization. A convicted
felon cannot play professional football. The devil's plans didn't fit
with God's plans for my son. Glory to God!

But the football prophecy, which hadn't come to fruition, ruled
over Mike's head. The ruling spirits assigned to take him out had
to give way to the prophecy. The judge allowed Mike to go to jail at
night and to track practice and school during the day! Mike's sentence was God telling him to choose whom he would serve. I thank

God that Mike made the right choice. Mike's supernatural shift in attitude came just in time.

IT COULD HAVE BEEN MY CHILD!

I read an alarming front-page article in the city newspaper that stated Michael's best friend had been arrested for murder. It was a story that shook my soul. For years I had been trying to keep Michael away from this young man. For the sake of confidentiality, I'll call him Eric.

Eric and my son Michael were childhood friends. Their fathers were also childhood friends, so the soul ties went way back. Michael and Eric grew apart when we moved overseas. After we returned to the States, we found out that Eric had stolen my son's identity and had committed crimes in Michael's name. At the time the police stopped him, he was perpetrating himself as Michael. I had to really believe that God would clear Michael's name.

> I WAS SLINGING OIL AND PLEADING, *THE BLOOD OF JESUS!* I MADE UP MY MIND THAT THE DEVIL COULD NOT HAVE MY CHILD. THE STATE'S ATTORNEY, LAWYERS, AND PROFESSIONALS INVOLVED SWORE THAT MY SON WOULD DO AT LEAST THREE YEARS AS A CONVICTED FELON. DESPITE THEIR PREDICTIONS, THE HAND OF GOD INTERVENED. IT WAS DIVINE DESTINY!

One day I met Eric in a store. His face looked deep and dark, and I had to look hard to find the little boy I once knew, but he was there. Eric was hard and very disrespectful, but I had made up my mind to deal with him. He had grown accustomed to having no respect for elders, so I demanded that he call me ma'am.

I told him that if he continued to steal my son's identity to commit crime, I would do to him what the FBI wouldn't do. He was shocked that I was not afraid of him.

He was so hard that I had to prophesy the little boy out of him. I told him that if he did not change, I saw him doing life in prison or getting a death sentence. I also prophesied about his two children and how it was not the will of God for them to visit him behind bars. Tears welled up in his eyes. I saw the little boy I once knew for the first time in a long time.

The demon spirit that controlled his life bowed for a minute and allowed the Eric I once knew as a boy to come out. I hugged him and told him that I loved him. I explained that I did not want him around my son until he changed his ways. Eric called Michael immediately after I left and told him what I said to him really touched him. Eric is now facing a death row sentence.

Another childhood friend of Eric and Michael—who happens to be my bestfriend's son—is also facing a death row sentence for murder. The seriousness of these two young men's situations made me fall on my face and say, "God, that could have been *my* child!" Against all the odds, my son is a free man today without a felony record. I know he's been delivered to fulfill his destiny.

GOD AND THE NFL

The verse that has helped me to endure whatever my son has been through says those who wait on the Lord will not be ashamed. The Greek translation of the word *ashamed* is *boosh*. It means that those who wait on the Lord will not be damned or cursed.

God watches over His promises to us as long as we do not take the position to watch over them for Him. Mike finally put the blessing on one mountain and the curse on the other. I know he will never forget the time he spent his nights in jail and his days as a college student and athlete. He made it, because God challenged him to choose whom he would serve.

After sixty days in jail, God delivered a new boy to me. Some of you mothers may not understand, but I thank Jesus for his jail time. My son's attitude did a 180-degree turn. He learned to appreciate so much and took nothing for granted!

Mike moved home with me for one year. It was as if he was in high school again. I told him where to go and not to go. He was twenty-three, and many people didn't understand his obedience to me. They said I needed to let him go on his own. I shut my ears to the voice of man and tuned to what the Holy Ghost was saying concerning my son.

God knew what was best for Michael. We settled some issues between us and agreed that we would wait on God. I even bought him a football video game so he could learn the rules of pro football. He was very gifted, but he had no football experience under his belt. During his stay, I paid him to clean my house, and he worked out in anticipation of getting a break in the NFL.

For one year he sat in front of the television playing *Madden NFL*, cleaned house, and worked out. Finally, he received a call to go to the NFL tryout camps in Europe. The first year he was cut, because he was not allocated, meaning no NFL team would sponsor him. The second year he barely got in. A coach promised to get him into the NFL Europe draft, but at the last minute told him it would not happen.

TRUSTING GOD

The draft had already closed, and the man failed to make good on his word. Michael was devastated, because he trusted this coach so much. I was in Barbados when Michael called me with the news. For the first time I could feel the pain he felt. I didn't have words for him, so I said nothing.

God quickly spoke to me and told me to get off to myself. We were staying near the beach, and as I heard the waters crashing against the rocks, I broke down in tears. I began to cry out to God for Mike. God told me to get my book *From a Mess to a Miracle* and read the chapter I had written concerning my son. The chapter reminded me of all the promises of God.

God told me that Mike's circumstances were not about him; they were about God's promises to me. When I gave up my track career, God told me that if I walked off the field, He would send my seed where I did not go.

Michael had been to San Francisco, the same city in which I decided to obey God and leave track forever. He also went to junior college where I became the national junior college champion. He finally ended up at Florida State University where I graduated and set records.

My spirit quickened, and I knew God was not finished with Michael and the NFL. The Lord spoke to me clearly to get my Bible and read Isaiah 49. When I read the chapter, it became like a healing balm to my soul. Verse 23 assured me that those who wait on the Lord would not be put to shame.

God let me know that we were not cursed, because we were obedient and had waited on Him. My favorite part of the scripture was that God had not forgotten me. In Isaiah 49:16, the Amplified version of the Bible, God said He had tattooed a picture of me in the palm of His hands. The verse also said the children of my bereavement would break out from their confined areas and beg for room to live.

God showed me the things that Michael was going through were because of my sins and that I had to continue to fight. I had to let my good seed override the bad. I called my son and told him to get ready; God was about to move for him. The next morning NFL Europe drafted him despite his inexperience with football.

Michael went to the trial camp with faith that he would make the team this time. All of the players were allocated but Michael. A person who was not allocated financially by an NFL team sponsorship could not be selected. Finances from NFL teams supported the European League.

Michael drove to the camp in the same car he used when he would get in trouble. He wrote the words "ALLOCATED BY JESUS" in the back window. Initially, I thought that was a bad idea. I didn't want any attention drawn to this car. (Remember, it was the same car in which he had been arrested during past brushes with the law.)

Other players joked about the writing, but God got the last laugh. But camp life was very difficult for Mike, because he was truly an underdog. He was overlooked in practice, and it seemed as though he was not given a chance.

One day while I was preaching in Trinidad, Michael called me to discuss his frustration. I will never forget him asking me, "Momma, how can I have a chance if they will not even put me in to see what I can do?" The only thing I could say was all is well.

Many of the staff members asked the coach who drafted Michael why he did so. The coach couldn't answer himself! He just felt "led" to bring Michael to camp so that maybe a scout could see him because he could not make the team, and that was all Michael wanted. He wanted a chance to prove that he could be a successful NFL football player.

We were told that about only 1½ percent of the guys who made the NFL Europe team would be drafted into the NFL. Michael was on the bottom of the totem pole. But sometimes this is where God wants us to be so that in the end, He alone gets the glory. The Word of God declares the last shall be first!

A MANIFESTED PROMISE

Things did not look good for Michael, and they were not getting any better. I went to church to preach one night, and God took me to the Book of Exodus. He showed me how He led His people with a cloud by day and a fire by night. When Pharaoh was gaining ground on God's people, the Bible says that the cloud and the fire shifted. This was my word from the Lord.

The devil was gaining ground on us, but God was about to shift some things! When we cannot see God, it does not mean He is not with us. He will never leave us or forsake us. This is when our faith must kick in. Not only did God have the back of His people, but He also stood between them and their enemy. Glory to God!

Though the enemy looked like he was about to take Michael out, God was only shifting gears. I called my son and told him to hold his head up and to go out there and play ball, because God was with him.

The next day the Holy Ghost shifted the gears into drive. Michael told me he had the best practice of his life. Two days later Michael was on the field when a man called him by name: "Michael Jennings."

Mike approached him and the man said, "Son, there is no way you can make this team because you are not allocated." Mike told the man he understood, and the man responded, "When they cut you from this team, I will pick you up on my team." Michael asked the man his name. It was as if the heavens opened up when the man responded.

> THE DEVIL WAS GAINING GROUND ON US, BUT GOD WAS ABOUT TO SHIFT SOME THINGS! WHEN WE CANNOT SEE GOD, IT DOES NOT MEAN HE IS NOT WITH US. HE WILL NEVER LEAVE US OR FORSAKE US. THIS IS WHEN OUR FAITH MUST KICK IN.

"I am Bill Belichick, the head coach of the New England Patriots." (The 2004 Super Bowl champions!) Word spread around the NFL Europe Camp that Michael Jennings truly was allocated by Jesus!

When there was no slot for him in the natural realm, God created one in the spirit. The coach of the NFL Europe Camp called Michael into the room to cut him from the team. "Michael," he said, "we are releasing you from this team, but there is something greater in store for you!"

As Mike completed the necessary paperwork to be released from the NFL Europe Camp, the woman processing his paperwork asked him why was he so happy. She was used to sad faces. Before Mike could respond, a voice came out of the back of the room, "Haven't you heard? He is allocated by Jesus!"

Two days later Michael signed a contract with the New England Patriots. After he completed rookie camp, I was not surprised to see a special article that featured my son, Michael Jennings. God will take the last and make them first.

The headline of the Boston newspaper said, "Patriots Like Jennings Track Record." God has blessed my son to sign contracts with the San Francisco 49ers, the New England Patriots, the Baltimore Ravens, and the New York Giants. He spent the first couple of years in the NFL playing on practice teams, but we believed God would supernaturally intervene.

In 2003 and 2004, Michael missed the final cut for NFL Europe training camp, but in 2005 Mike has gone back to Europe *allocated by Jesus!* Mike, playing wide receiver for the New York Giants practice squad, was sent back to the NFL Europe by the Giants. He skipped the draft and went straight to becoming the number one pick for the World Bowl Champions, the Berlin Thunder, as a *starting wide receiver*. News reporters from Germany came to America to see his car, which had the saying "Allocated by Jesus" on it. Michael is now known as the number one wide receiver in the entire league.

NFL players often ask Michael the name of his college football team. When he tells them he has never played college ball, God always gets the glory! Everyone knows him as the pro-football player who had no experience. When something is part of your destiny, no experience is necessary!

CHAPTER 19

IT SHOULD'VE BEEN ME!

AS I LOOK back on my childhood years and realize the fate that many of my playmates received, my mind cannot help but think, *It should've been me!* Nothing separated me from the horrible things that I am about to share with you except the grace of God. I do not remember any of my neighborhood friends serving God, and rightfully, we were all guilty. Somehow God gave me clemency and was lenient with my soul when I did not deserve it. I will never forget my younger years in what we called "the woods." We had decent houses and it surely looked better than uptown, but a spirit of death traveled through our neighborhood. It was by the grace of God that this spirit passed over my door!

THE SPIRIT OF DEATH IN "THE WOODS"

I lived in the deep part of "the woods." The spirit of death stopped by many of the houses that were in walking distance of my home. This spirit manifests itself in more ways than natural death. It comes to steal, kill, or destroy. When it stops by a house, if it does not completely snuff out a life, then it sure makes that person wish he were dead.

The first house where this spirit stopped by was Johnny's house. He was the most popular boy on our block. All the girls liked him, and he was a great athlete. From the time he was teenager and into adulthood, he went to prison many times. While in prison, we had heard rumors that he acquired a taste for the homosexual lifestyle. I have never met a more gifted guy in my life. All of us wanted to be like Johnny when we were young, but something dark seemed to grow up with him. Johnny's life ended when he was brutally murdered on a street corner uptown. As his dead body lay in a puddle of blood, he was dressed in female clothing. Destruction manifests itself in many ways. The devil destroyed Johnny's manhood, and the lifestyle that came with it took him down a never-ending tunnel of destruction.

The next house the spirit of death visited was Carlton's house. He was popular for being unattractive. (At least, we thought so as little children.) Nobody would tell him to his face that he wasn't cute, because he was big, husky, and mean. I remember when I was a little girl he asked me to be his girlfriend. I did not dare say no! After I told him yes, I ran home crying, hoping that he would forget all about my vow. He never mentioned it again, which made my life in the neighborhood much easier. All of the men in Carlton's family were alcoholics, and the generational curse did not skip Carlton. He was a chronic alcoholic. Carlton landed a successful career, moved away from the city, and married a beautiful woman. Everyone was shocked! I guess beauty is in the eyes of the beholder. After his marriage ended in divorce, he returned to the neighborhood to start all over. The dark assignment against Carlton hid in the corridors and waited for the opportune moment to take him out. I saw Carlton at a neighborhood convenience store when I was visiting from the military. I was saved, and I told him that the Lord showed me that trouble was coming his way. He was sloppy drunk, and I sternly warned him that if he did not get his life right with Jesus, the devil was going to take him out. Less than a year later, he was imprisoned for rape. Rumors were that he was set up. Carlton received a very long sentence and is still incarcerated today. I love and miss Carlton because he was really a nice guy. But like I mentioned earlier, the death spirit manifests itself in many ways!

Derrick's story took everyone by surprise. He was a very fat, little boy who never bothered anyone. As a matter of fact, we used to beat him up all the time. Unfortunately, the enemy sent destruction to Derrick's life, too. After we graduated from high school, he became very sick. We were used to living a fast life, but we did not know very many sick children. We may not have had the best of things, but all of our friends were generally healthy. We were used to drug addiction, brothers and sisters going to prison, and family feuds, but death at a young age was a stranger in our community. Derrick died from a disease that we later found out he had at birth. None of us ever knew he was sick. The enemy also comes to steal! He stole Derrick's life at a young age. Nothing gives you a real picture of life like the reality of death! As hard as our lives may have seemed, this reality was hard to swallow.

The story of my next childhood friend is close to my heart. Ronnie was one of the guys in the neighborhood who never got in trouble. He served in the military overseas during my tour there. I tried to contact him while we were in Germany together. Before I could reach him, a friend contacted me to let me know that Ronnie was killed in a truck accident during Operation Desert Storm. This news hurt me, because I never got the opportunity to witness to him. My hope is that God sent another laborer. The spirit of death has the ability to follow and pursue its intended victim.

Though spirits operate territorially, there are many levels of devils in the dark hierarchy of the satanic kingdom. The satanic kingdom has no specific domain, and that is why Satan is called the god of this world. (See 2 Corinthians 4:4.) A spirit can trail its victim by assignment whether it is by generation, association, location, or incantation. Whenever a devil cannot cross a line to get its assigned

181

victim, it will pass the baton to the next demon of the region, family, or season. It is possible that the spirit of death assigned to Ronnie followed him to his tragic end overseas. The Bible teaches us that the devil seeks whom he may devour. (See 1 Peter 5:8.) After Ronnie's tragic death, a burden arose in my heart to reach out to my childhood friends. Since then, I have been in contact with many of them, and they are faithfully serving the Lord.

My last story is about Aikeem. I learned to fight in the streets by having brawls with Aikeem. No matter what we faced, Aikeem and I always settled it with our fists. Aikeem could never keep a full-time job. Eventually, he became a full-time drug addict. He also had a serious alcohol problem, and I would often see him being thrown out of my father's bars. Aikeem's appearance was that of a homeless person. His mother, brothers, and sisters were a strong support system, but it is difficult to support someone who does not have a will to stand. Aikeem got so bad that I began to be afraid of him when I saw him on the streets. It seemed as if he had lost his mind, and he talked like the crazy, old men that hung out uptown. The last time I saw him I knew that he did not have long if he continued down the path he was going.

The Bible also says the enemy comes to kill (John 10:10). The definition for the word *kill* is to "deprive of life" and "to cause to cease operating." When I looked into Aikeem's eyes, there was no life. He was walking around as if he was living, but he had ceased to operate as a human being. This is the reason why Jesus came—to give us abundant life!

It was rumored that Aikeem had AIDS. All of his symptoms lined up with the rumor. As bad as Aikeem's situation was, he did not want anything to do with Jesus, and he forcefully avoided anyone who witnessed to him. One day, one of my ministers at Spoken Word was ministering at the hospital. He felt led to pray for people on their deathbeds. As he was walking down the hall of the hospital, he saw a woman who seemed to be troubled. As this minister comforted the woman, she told him her son was dying and would not accept the

Lord. I thank Jesus that the troubled woman was Aikeem's mom!

The minister went to Aikeem's room to minister to him. Because the minister was from our neighborhood, Aikeem recognized him and responded well! My minister friend never knew that the Lord was using him to answer my prayers. Aikeem accepted Christ that hour and went to be with the Lord a few hours later. Death had no sting and the grave had no victory in Aikeem's life. Though Aikeem had bouts with the spirit of death in his life, in death he received victory over the Grim Reaper. His mother is a saved woman who had cried out in prayer for her son's soul for years. The effectual fervent prayers of the righteous avail much. (See James 5:16.) There is nothing like the prayer of a mother for her child!

> ALL OF THESE STORIES SHOW HOW IT NOT ONLY *COULD HAVE BEEN ME,* BUT IT ALSO *SHOULD'VE BEEN ME!*

My minister friend called to give the testimony about the strange man that he had led to the Lord on his deathbed. Minutes later my sister called to tell me that Aikeem had passed away. It was not long before the Holy Ghost allowed me to put two and two together. This was no strange man; God had saved my childhood friend! Although he suffered in life and died an untimely death, he was ushered into the presence of the Lord. Praise God! What clemency! Many would say that God is not fair because Aikeem did not live a life for the Lord. But at the last minute, Aikeem made it to glory!

All of these stories show how it not only *could have been me,* but it also *should've been me!* I deserved what some of my friends received—and more—but I was spared by the grace of God. God did not spare me because I was more special than anyone. He spared all because of His wonderful grace! Grace is an unexplainable state of being protected and sanctified by the favor of God.

It was grace that healed the man at the pool of Bethesda. There were five porches (entrances), and he was lying in the right one because of grace. There were multitudes of sick people, but Grace commanded that he take up his bed and walk while others remained lame. David had five smooth stones but with the grace of God, he used one of the stones to kill his strong enemy. Five is the number of grace, and I do not think it is by chance. Grace is the five

> JESUS CAME TO THE WORLD SO THAT THOSE WHO CHOOSE TO RECEIVE HIM MAY HAVE ABUNDANT LIFE ON EARTH AND ETERNAL LIFE WITH HIM.

fingers of God covering space that we do not have so that we can pass over! It was grace that caused the death spirit to pass by the children of Israel so that their firstborn would not be destroyed. I thank God that the Grim Reaper passed by my house in "the woods," and I give Jesus the glory for it.

Yes, the Grim Reaper hung out in "the woods," but where sin and death abound, grace does much more abound! When Jesus shed His blood on Calvary, that was grace! And that grace has given us victory over death, hell, and the grave. Jesus came to the world so that those who choose to receive Him may have abundant life on earth and eternal life with Him.

There are times my heart gets heavy when I think about the fate of my playmates. But at the same time, my spirit rejoices as I praise God for deliverance, because it should've been me!

THE WALKING DEAD

Today, when I ride down the streets of my city, I see how crack has taken its toll on the lives of people I grew up with. They look like the walking dead! I dare not judge them because when I look at them, I see me without Jesus!

A few years ago one of the prettiest girls in our school was found dead, face down in a ditch. It was her fate as a result of the lifestyle she chose as a drug addict.

The last time I saw her she was hiding in my stepmother's yard. My stepmother lived next to a dock where people parked to smoke dope. This girl was in the yard, having a bowel movement with no shame. It was as if she were an animal.

As she was stooping, she looked over at me, with her finger over her mouth, saying, "Shhhhh, they are going to hear you!" Crack had taken her mind. At that time, I had never seen anyone on drugs or experienced it for myself. I did not understand! Little did I know that one day I would.

By God's grace and mercy, the curse of the walking dead was broken off of my life. Some of those young ladies whom I considered my good friends at one time now beat on my car window begging for a dollar for drugs.

Sometimes they come to the church to try and beat us out of money. It is hard for me to get mad at them because I keep remembering that it could have been me. It seems as if the free-basing era of smoking cocaine took out an entire generation. The dope of this era is crack, which is free-base cocaine with added chemicals. These chemicals are said to speed up the deterioration of the brain and to take addicts out quicker. Most real crack heads in our city range in age from thirty-five to sixty years old. These were the "freebasers." This was the generation to experiment with smoking cocaine. Before this generation, many did not know what the long-term results of crack addiction were. So now we know! This is the generation of the "walking dead."

I thank God that the next generation has a better chance! The warning to them is the sign of their mothers and fathers that grope around like the curse described in the Book of Deuteronomy:

> And thou shall grope at noonday, as the blind gropes in
> darkness, and thou shalt not prosper in thy ways: and thou
> shalt be only oppressed and spoiled evermore, and no man
> shall save thee....And among these nations shalt thou find
> no ease, neither shall the sole of thy foot have rest: but the
> LORD shall give thee there a trembling heart, and failing of
> eyes and sorrow of mind: And thy life shall hang in doubt
> before thee; and thou shalt fear day and night, and shalt
> have no assurance of thy life.
> —DEUTERONOMY 28:29, 65–66, KJV

These are surely the manifestations of the walking dead. Today, I
rarely pray for young people on crack; most of the crackheads are
of my generation. There is a new strongman for this era. Nowa-
days, most young people deal drugs and do not abuse them. The
ironic thing is that these young people cry out for help for their
mothers, fathers, and older relatives, never realizing that they are
part of the problem.

Everybody in our community has been affected by drug addiction in some way. If they were not strung out, someone in their
family or neighborhood is. When I preach in prisons in Florida, so
many men and women are there who were my good friends. I am
not one to cry too much, but when I go to these prisons, I always
break down in tears. When I see behind bars the faces of the people
with whom I once ran the streets, I cannot help but see me! Abundant life in Christ is the only thing that will break the curse of the
walking dead.

THE GOOD NEWS!

The good news is that many of my other friends and relatives
whom I considered among the walking dead are now free and serving God. My father, Perk, has also given his life to the Lord. As I
write this book, he is suffering from physical ailments, but he has
confessed Jesus as Savior! I never thought I would see this day. My
family and friends who have not given their lives to the Lord know

where to come when they are ready—Spoken Word Ministries on the corner of Steele and Blue!

They have watched the fruit of what God has done in me over the years. God has given me a reputation on the streets that has opened the hearts of many to receive Him. These people cannot relate to the typical "status quo Christianity." I thank Him so much for allowing me to stand in the gap to make up the hedge in the darkest parts of my city. Salvation and deliverance are also touching the lives of my husband's family through Spoken Word. My husband, Danny (most people know him as Ardell), used to bring dope to his family reunions. Danny now preaches the gospel, gets people filled with the Holy Ghost, and casts out devils at the family reunions. The good news is taking over the lives of our family members and friends. Even the walking dead are being raised!

CHAPTER 20

FROM THE GUTTERMOST
TO THE UTTERMOST

DANNY AND I have been married for many years now. Between the two of us, we have six children. God gave us double for our trouble concerning the baby we lost to cocaine. The first year of our marriage I got pregnant with twins, Elijah and Elisha. At the time of this writing, the twins are seven years old and headed for Hollywood to do sitcoms this year. I prophesied that they would go to Hollywood when they were eighteen months old.

The church on Steele and Blue has blossomed over the past seven years. Though our congregation is around four hundred members, God has given us international exposure, and people from around the world visit us every year. Visitors from China, England, the Netherlands, Africa, and many other countries show up at our church for a regular service, and they come to be delivered by the supernatural power of God.

We take teams to different nations around the world to teach, train, and activate ministries in warfare and deliverance. My husband and

I have traveled back and forth to twelve countries over the past few years. We've been to Hong Kong, Malaysia, Croatia, Japan, Germany, England, South Africa, Trinidad, Barbados, China, Canada, and South Korea. We've declined invitations from at least ten other countries because our schedules will not permit us to go.

I have written four books, and I am currently an author with Charisma House of Strang Communications. My last book, *Clean House Strong House*, was nominated best book in the charismatic category by the Christian Retailers' Choice Award. More than twenty thousand copies were sold in less than a year. I am also a regular columnist for *Charisma* and *SpiritLed Woman* magazines.

> OUR SUCCESS RATE IN MODIFYING THE BEHAVIOR OF DRUG ADDICTS, DEALERS, AND PEOPLE WITH OTHER ADVERSE LIFESTYLES HAS BEEN SO EFFECTIVE IN OUR CITY THAT IT GOT THE ATTENTION OF OUR LOCAL GOVERNMENT.

God has blessed both Danny and me to meet mighty men and women of God. I met Derek Prince in England at a conference where we were both speaking a few years before his death. He was physically weak, so he sat in a chair, teaching. My heart rejoiced to sit under such a mighty pioneer.

I was honored when Derek Prince came to my workshop session. God gave me a word of knowledge about his sickness, and God supernaturally healed him in the service. I was later asked to endorse a biography about Derek Prince's life.

But one of the greatest honors we have is to serve under the leadership of Apostle John Eckhardt of Crusaders Ministry in Chicago, Illinois. Apostle Eckhardt was a key asset in launching the foundation of our international ministry.

We recently flew to Washington DC to participate in a press conference on Capitol Hill. We met with other leaders to discuss the issue of same-sex marriage. It was a blessing to think that God would take me from the "crack house" to the House of Representatives.

God has also opened crazy doors for our home church. CeCe Winans chose Spoken Word Ministries to sponsor her Throne Room Tour over the requests of several megachurches in our area. Thousands came to worship God and be set free. I am involved in international conferences with the End-Time Handmaidens sponsored by Gwen Shaw. She is a pioneer for intercession around the world, and her events represent prayer warriors from more than 150 nations.

Most of the doors to ministry that have opened for us in recent years have been because of the support we have received from our friends, Stephen and Joy Strang, the founders and publishers of *Charisma* and *SpiritLed Woman* magazines. God has even touched their hearts to make us the conveners of a major conference they have sponsored over the last ten years where nearly nine thousand women, and some men, have attended. As of April 2005, Spoken Word Ministries will be the host.

As I am writing this chapter, I am on my way to meet with a representative from the mayor's office in our city. The mayor's office contacted us to give us government money to "do what we do." Our success rate in modifying the behavior of drug addicts, dealers, and people with other adverse lifestyles has been so effective in our city that it got the attention of our local government.

Finally, God blew our minds when He took us to a country and in a sense set us before kings as the prophets have prophesied unto us. We were escorted to the financial capital of the world to prophesy over the world finances. We decreed that the wealth of the wicked would be transferred to the just as Scripture has told. This venture gave us audience with several billionaires who are in the top twenty-five wealthiest people in the world. We prophesied to them, got them filled with the Holy Ghost, and cast out devils.

One financial tycoon was miraculously healed by the awesome power of God, and the word of that healing spread like fire. We were escorted to the home of one of the top ten government officials of that country. By God's grace, we prophesied with accuracy the present state of government affairs. Beyond our knowledge, the things we prophesied were highlights in the national papers. As my husband and I were escorted by high-level security officials everywhere we went, I would smile at the devil every now and then, thinking, *How you like me now!* Because we were the guests of the richest and most famous people in the country, the red carpet was rolled out everywhere we went. Our friends owned the largest buildings, malls, hotels, and businesses in the nation. Every need that we had was immediately met. My armorbearer on this trip was a millionaire. She and her husband own one of the largest clothing manufacturing companies in the world. They own three factories. As we prayed through their business offices, we made arrangements to start our own clothing line—D-Busters, short for Demon Busters. The emblem is a picture of a foot kicking the devil in his backside. To God be the glory!

While working on this book, as a result of a test that I took, the doctors were summoning me to come in to take a second look at "something that was not right" in my left breast. I got these results twice over the past three years. The devil tried to speak to my mind and say that two different doctors could not be wrong. The Holy Ghost told me not to allow them to diagnose me.

One of my close friends who worked on *Delivered to Destiny* with me called crying the day after we completed the project. Her mom was diagnosed with cancer. As the doctor's office pleaded with me to come back to see if I had cancer, I prayed with my friend's mom with all my heart and prophesied that all would be well. I boarded a plane for the international trip that I have been speaking of above and did not share my situation with my family or closest friends.

To my surprise, the Lord had me share my situation with my armorbearer who owned the clothing factories. I had no idea why, but God knew that her good friend was the chief of nuclear medicine at the largest hospital in the country. He is one of the number one cancer specialists in the world. Within one hour after sharing with her, I was rushed to his hospital. He met me in the parking lot and escorted me in.

I was immediately prepared for a test that normally had a two-year waiting period and diagnosed with equipment that is the newest technology worldwide. A picture was taken of every organ in my body, and a team of doctors analyzed my body on computer screens that looked like pictures of the bionic woman. This was done in a twenty-four hour period! When I returned home, my friend called and said that when her mom had went back to the doctor to start treatment, NO CANCER WAS FOUND! The result is that I received a clean bill of health! I thank God for His supernatural intervention.

It would have been better if the devil had never sent the arrow, because now God gets the glory! Isaiah 29:6–8 tells of how the Lord will deliver us from the snare of the enemy. This passage declares that the attacks of the enemy will be like a dream passed away. God says that the devil will be like a hungry man dreaming that he is eating, but he will wake up hungry. God rebukes the devourer on our behalf.

So as you have read what I have come out of, do not drop a tear on my behalf. I take pleasure in going through trouble so that I can come out victorious. Trouble perfects our praise. Psalm 67:5 tells us that when we praise God, the earth yields her increase. Ezekiel 34:26 says that God will make the places around our hill a blessing and will cause the shower to come down in His season. When the "shower" releases "His" blessings and the "earth" yields "her" increase, spiritual procreation takes place. All of creation has to line up with the will of God for our lives, and we can be translated from the guttermost to the uttermost.

I have made the confession on the next page at every worship service at Spoken Word since the ministry began. Though none of these words lined up with my life at the time, I confessed them. I have seen God make things that were not become as though they were. It is my prayer that this confession will bless you! I'm outta here!

—KIM DANIELS

MY CONFESSION OF FAITH

THIS CONFESSION OF faith has been a blessing to me ever since our church services began. We have never had a service without declaring these words. I pray this confession will be a blessing to you and yours!

I am a child of the King, an heir of God, and a joint heir with Christ. I am more than a conqueror through Him that loves me. Fear has no place in my life, because God has not given me a spirit of fear. I am confident that no weapon formed against me will prosper, because God is for me. Who can be against me?

Every curse spoken against me is to no avail, because I am blessed. Satan cannot curse whom God has blessed. I am blessed coming in and blessed going out. My enemies shall come up against me in one way, but God will cause them to flee in seven ways. All that I set my hands to do will prosper. All the people of the earth shall see that I am called by the name of the Lord.

The Lord has made me plenteous in goods. I am a lender and not a borrower. I am the head and not the tail. I am above only and not beneath. *I am persuaded that neither death, nor life, nor angels, nor principalities, nor powers, nor things present, nor things to come, nor height, nor depth, nor any other creature shall be able to separate me from the love of God.*